EYEWITNESS VISUAL DICTIONARIES

THE VISUAL
DICTIONARY *of*
DINOSAURS

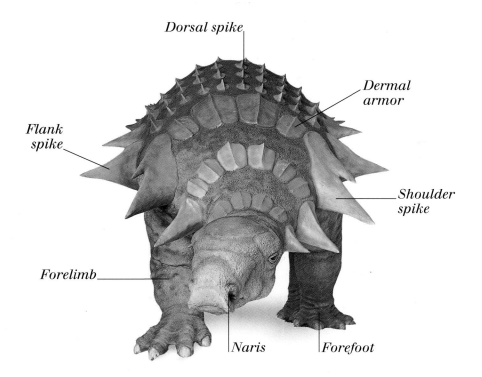

Dorsal spike

Dermal armor

Flank spike

Shoulder spike

Forelimb

Naris

Forefoot

**EXTERNAL FEATURES
OF EDMONTONIA**

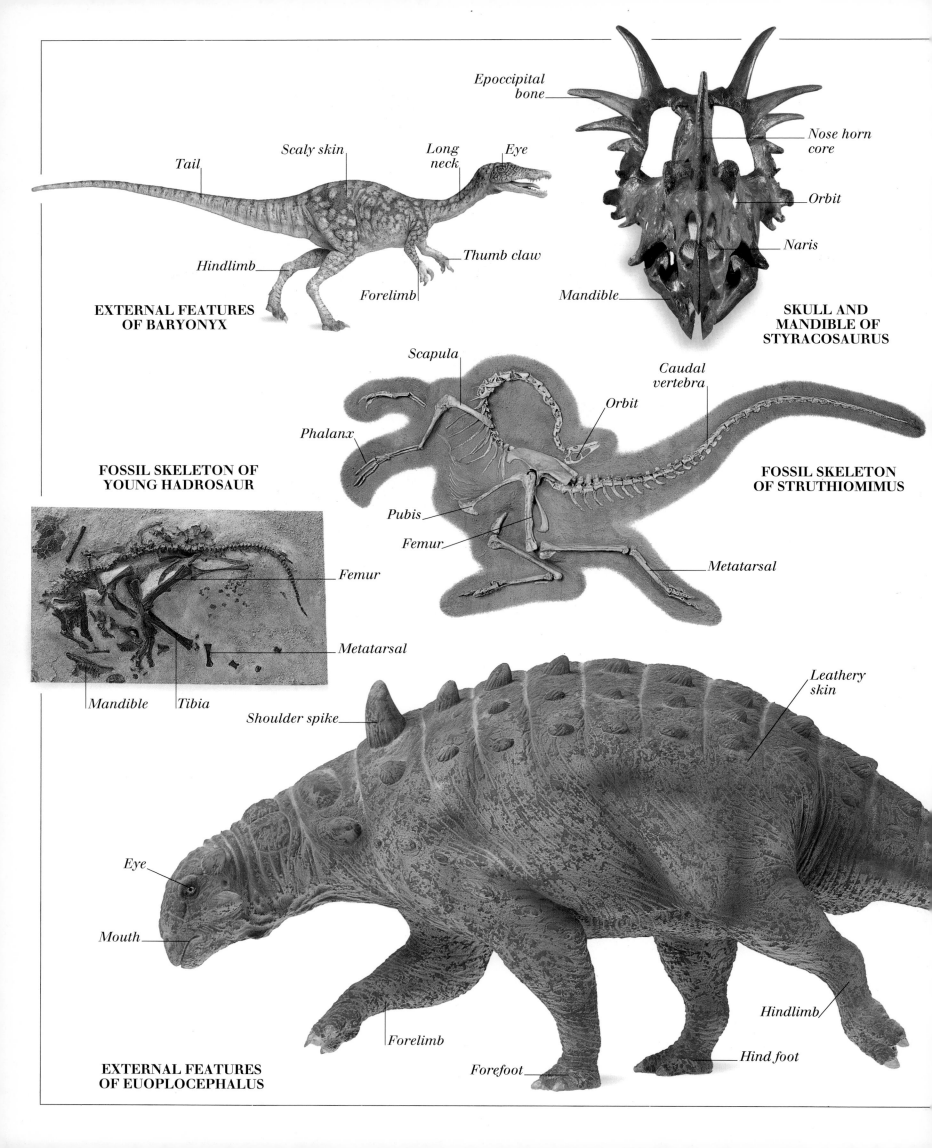

**EXTERNAL FEATURES
OF BARYONYX**

Tail

Scaly skin

Long
neck

Eye

Hindlimb

Thumb claw

Forelimb

**SKULL AND
MANDIBLE OF
STYRACOSAURUS**

Epoccipital
bone

Nose horn
core

Orbit

Naris

Mandible

**FOSSIL SKELETON OF
YOUNG HADROSAUR**

Scapula

Phalanx

Orbit

Caudal
vertebra

**FOSSIL SKELETON
OF STRUTHIOMIMUS**

Pubis

Femur

Metatarsal

Femur

Metatarsal

Mandible

Tibia

Shoulder spike

Leathery
skin

Eye

Mouth

Hindlimb

Hind foot

Forelimb

Forefoot

**EXTERNAL FEATURES
OF EUOPLOCEPHALUS**

EYEWITNESS VISUAL DICTIONARIES

THE VISUAL
DICTIONARY *of*
DINOSAURS

*Emerged
hatchling*

Eggshell

*Nest
material*

MODEL OF ORODROMEUS NEST

Tail

Tail club

DK PUBLISHING, INC

WWW.DK.COM

A DK PUBLISHING BOOK

WWW.DK.COM

PROJECT ART EDITOR CLARE SHEDDEN
DESIGNER ELLEN WOODWARD

PROJECT EDITORS FIONA COURTENAY-THOMPSON, MARY LINDSAY
CONSULTANT EDITORS DAVID LAMBERT, DR. RALPH E. MOLNAR
U.S. CONSULTANT LOWELL DINGUS (AMERICAN MUSEUM OF NATURAL HISTORY)
U.S. EDITOR CHARLES A. WILLS

MANAGING ART EDITOR STEPHEN KNOWLDEN
SENIOR EDITOR MARTYN PAGE
MANAGING EDITOR RUTH MIDGLEY

PHOTOGRAPHY ANDY CRAWFORD
ILLUSTRATIONS JOHN TEMPERTON, GRAHAM ROSEWARNE
MODEL MAKERS JOHN HOLMES, ROBY BRAUN, GRAHAM HIGH AND JEREMY HUNT (CENTAUR STUDIOS)

PRODUCTION HILARY STEPHENS

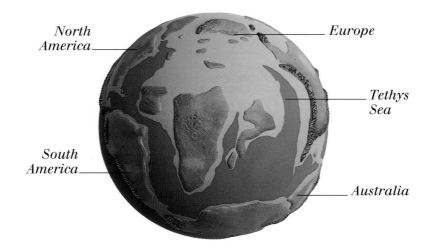

North America — Europe

Tethys Sea

South America — Australia

THE EARTH DURING THE CRETACEOUS PERIOD

FIRST AMERICAN EDITION, 1993

8 10 9

Published in the United States by DK Publishing, Inc.
95 Madison Avenue, New York, New York 10016

LIBRARY OF CONGRESS CATALOGING-IN-PUBLICATION DATA

Dinosaurs. — 1st American ed.
p. cm. — (Eyewitness visual dictionaries)
Includes index.
Summary: Text and labeled illustrations present the different
types of dinosaurs and their anatomy.
ISBN 1-56458-188-8
1. Dinosaurs—Terminology—Juvenile literature.
2. Dinosaurs—Pictorial works—Juvenile literature.
3. Picture dictionaries, English—Juvenile literature.
[1. Dinosaurs.] I. Series
QE862.D5D5173 1993
567. 9'1'03—dc20   92-53446
                                                          CIP
                                                          AC

REPRODUCED BY COLOURSCAN, SINGAPORE
PRINTED AND BOUND IN SPAIN BY ARTES GRÁFICAS TOLEDO S.A.U.
D.L. TO: 7-2001

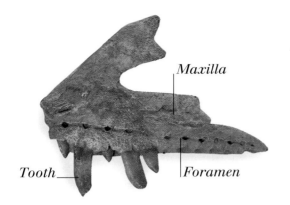

Maxilla

Tooth

Foramen

UPPER JAW OF TERATOSAURUS

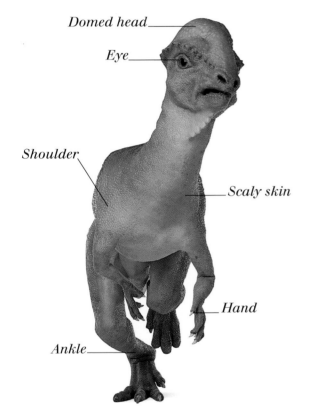

Domed head

Eye

Shoulder

Scaly skin

Hand

Ankle

EXTERNAL FEATURES OF STEGOCERAS

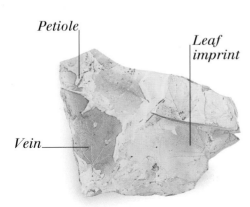

Petiole

Leaf imprint

Vein

FOSSILIZED LEAF OF CRETACEOUS TREE

Contents

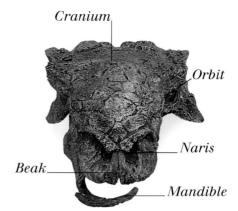

Cranium

Orbit

Naris

Beak

Mandible

SKULL AND MANDIBLE OF EUOPLOCEPHALUS

Eye

Whiplike tail

Long neck

Forelimb

EXTERNAL FEATURES OF BAROSAURUS

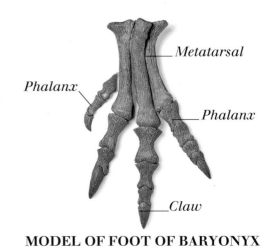

Metatarsal

Phalanx

Phalanx

Claw

MODEL OF FOOT OF BARYONYX

The dinosaurs

DINOSAURS WERE A LARGE GROUP OF REPTILES that were the dominant land vertebrates (animals with backbones) on Earth from the first part of the Late Triassic (231 million years ago) to the end of the Cretaceous period (65 million years ago). Dinosaurs were diverse, ranging from huge herbivores (plant-eaters) such as *Barosaurus*, which was 90 ft (27.4 m) long, to small carnivores (flesh-eaters) such as *Compsognathus*, which was less than 4 ft 8 in (1.4 m) long. Two features that most dinosaurs had in common were raised metatarsals and an erect stance. Their erect stance enabled dinosaurs to keep their bodies well above the ground, unlike the sprawling and semi-sprawling stances of other reptiles. Dinosaurs can be categorized into two main groups according to the structure of their pelvis (hip bones): ornithischian (bird-hipped) and saurischian (lizard-hipped) dinosaurs. Ornithischians had a relatively long, shallow ilium and a backward-slanting pubis. Most saurischians had a shorter, deeper ilium and a forward-slanting pubis. A third, small group of dinosaurs, the herrerasaurs, had pelvic bones similar to those of saurischians.

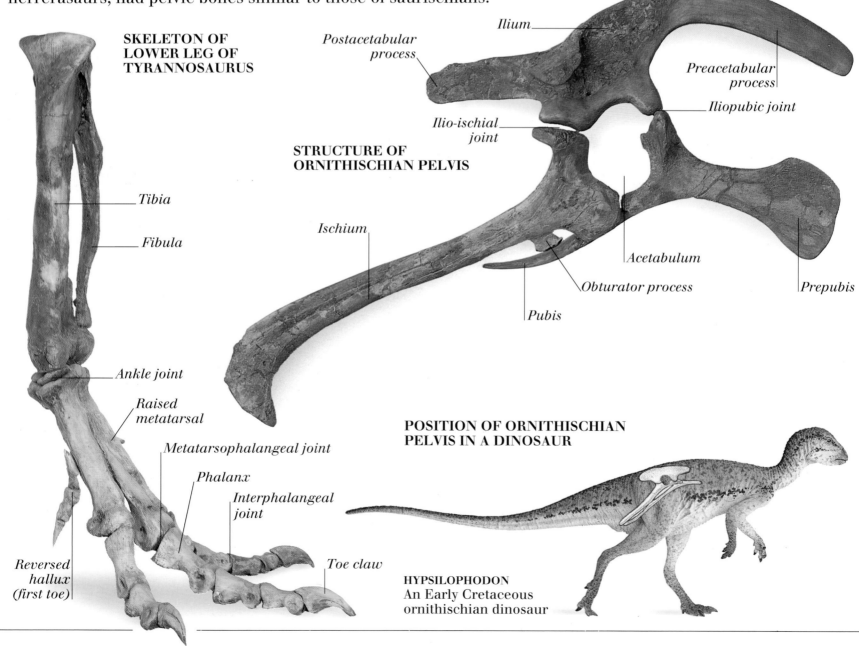

COMPARISON OF ANIMAL STANCES

BAROSAURUS
A saurischian dinosaur

ERECT STANCE
The thighs and upper arms project straight down from the body, so that the knees and elbows are straight.

SKELETON OF LOWER LEG OF TYRANNOSAURUS

Tibia

Fibula

Ankle joint

Raised metatarsal

Metatarsophalangeal joint

Phalanx

Interphalangeal joint

Reversed hallux (first toe)

Toe claw

STRUCTURE OF ORNITHISCHIAN PELVIS

Ilium

Postacetabular process

Preacetabular process

Iliopubic joint

Ilio-ischial joint

Ischium

Acetabulum

Obturator process

Pubis

Prepubis

POSITION OF ORNITHISCHIAN PELVIS IN A DINOSAUR

HYPSILOPHODON
An Early Cretaceous ornithischian dinosaur

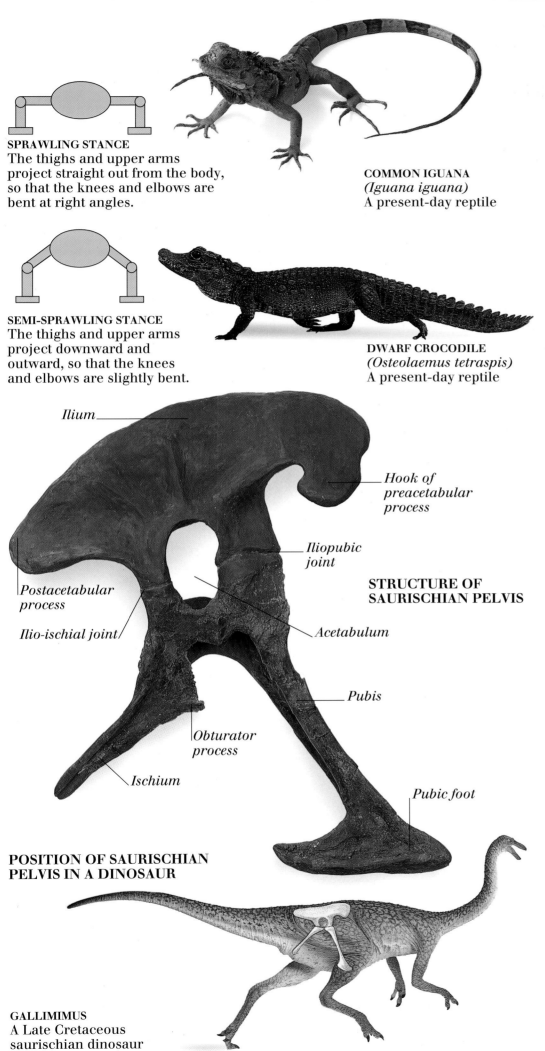

SPRAWLING STANCE
The thighs and upper arms project straight out from the body, so that the knees and elbows are bent at right angles.

COMMON IGUANA
(Iguana iguana)
A present-day reptile

SEMI-SPRAWLING STANCE
The thighs and upper arms project downward and outward, so that the knees and elbows are slightly bent.

DWARF CROCODILE
(Osteolaemus tetraspis)
A present-day reptile

Ilium

Hook of preacetabular process

Iliopubic joint

STRUCTURE OF SAURISCHIAN PELVIS

Postacetabular process

Ilio-ischial joint

Acetabulum

Pubis

Obturator process

Ischium

Pubic foot

POSITION OF SAURISCHIAN PELVIS IN A DINOSAUR

GALLIMIMUS
A Late Cretaceous saurischian dinosaur

THE GEOLOGICAL TIMESCALE

MYA	PERIOD		ERA
2	QUATERNARY		CENOZOIC
	TERTIARY		CENOZOIC
65	CRETACEOUS		MESOZOIC
144	JURASSIC		MESOZOIC
208	TRIASSIC		MESOZOIC
248	PERMIAN		PALEOZOIC
286	CARBONIFEROUS	PENNSYLVANIAN (NORTH AMERICA)	PALEOZOIC
320		MISSISSIPPIAN (NORTH AMERICA)	PALEOZOIC
360	DEVONIAN		PALEOZOIC
408	SILURIAN		PALEOZOIC
438	ORDOVICIAN		PALEOZOIC
505	CAMBRIAN		PALEOZOIC
550	PRECAMBRIAN TIME		
4600			

Triassic period

CRETACEOUS 144-65 MYA	
JURASSIC 208-144 MYA	MESOZOIC ERA
TRIASSIC 248-208 MYA	

THE TRIASSIC PERIOD (248–208 million years ago) marked the beginning of what is known as the Age of the Dinosaurs (the Mesozoic era). During this period, the present-day continents were massed together, forming one huge continent known as Pangaea. This landmass experienced extremes of climate, with lush green areas around the coast or by lakes and rivers, and arid deserts in the interior. The only forms of plant life were nonflowering plants, such as conifers, ferns, cycads, and ginkgos; flowering plants had not yet evolved. The principal forms of animal life included primitive amphibians, rhynchosaurs ("beaked lizards"), and primitive crocodilians. Dinosaurs first appeared about 230 million years ago, at the beginning of the Late Triassic. The earliest known dinosaurs were the carnivorous (flesh-eating) herrerasaurids and staurikosaurids, such as *Herrerasaurus* and *Staurikosaurus*. Early herbivorous (plant-eating) dinosaurs first appeared in the Late Triassic and included *Plateosaurus* and *Technosaurus*. By the end of the Triassic, dinosaurs dominated Pangaea, possibly contributing to the extinction of many other reptiles.

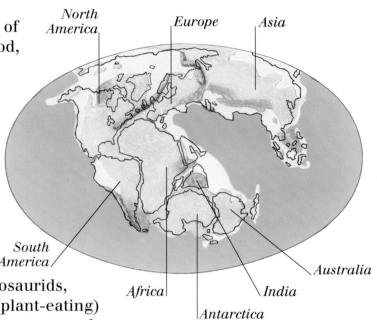

North America
Europe
Asia
South America
Africa
Antarctica
India
Australia

EXAMPLES OF TRIASSIC PLANT GROUPS

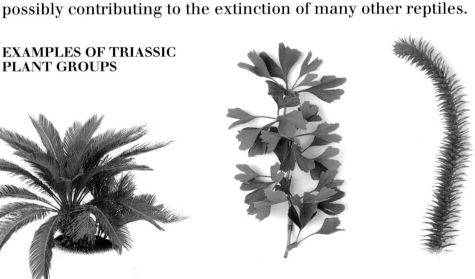

A PRESENT-DAY CYCAD
(*Cycas revoluta*)

A PRESENT-DAY GINKGO
(*Ginkgo biloba*)

A PRESENT-DAY CONIFER
(*Araucaria araucana*)

AN EXTINCT FERN
(*Pachypteris* sp.)

AN EXTINCT CYCAD
(*Cycas* sp.)

EXAMPLES OF TRIASSIC DINOSAURS

STAURIKOSAURUS
A staurikosaurid
Length: 6 ft 6 in (2 m)

COELOPHYSIS
A coelophysid
Length: 10 ft (3 m)

TECHNOSAURUS
A primitive ornithischian
Length: 3 ft 3 in (1 m)

PLATEOSAURUS
A plateosaurid
Length: 26 ft (7.9 m)

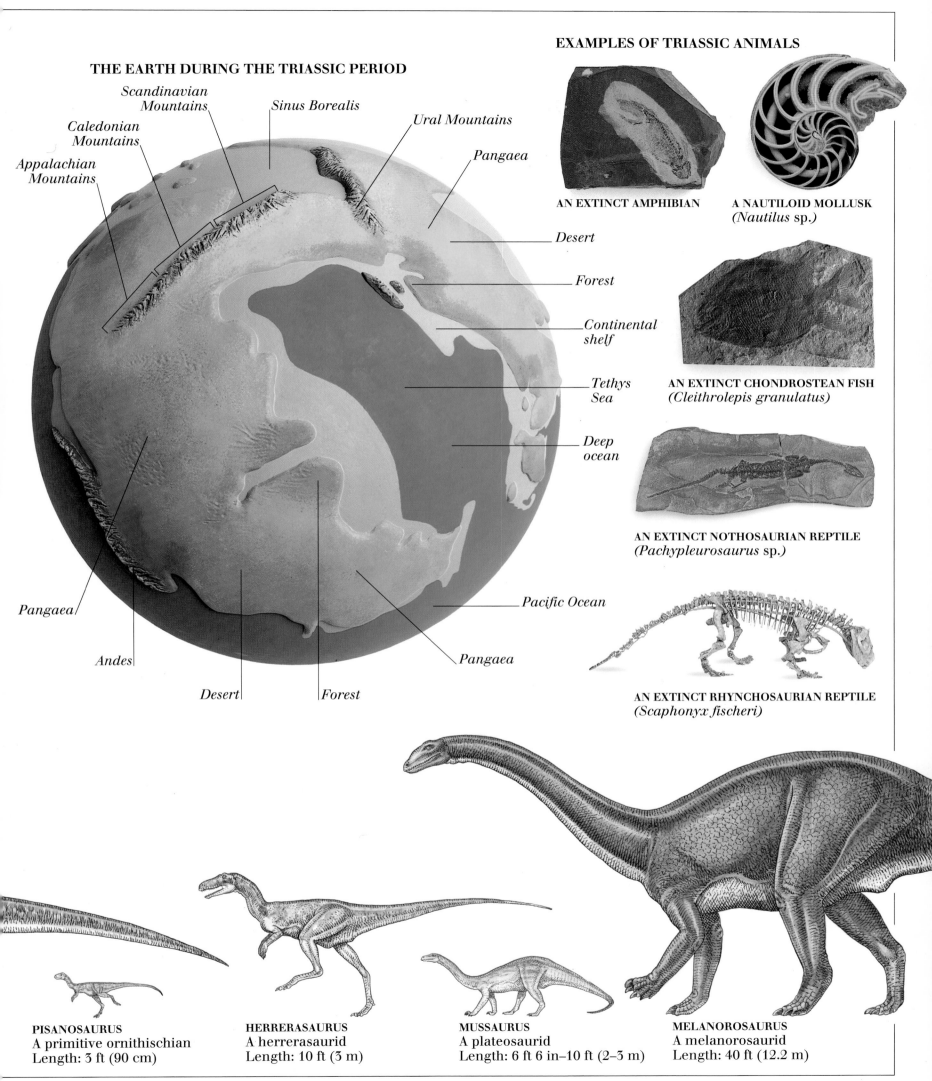

THE EARTH DURING THE TRIASSIC PERIOD

Appalachian
Mountains

Caledonian
Mountains

Scandinavian
Mountains

Sinus Borealis

Ural Mountains

Pangaea

Desert

Forest

Continental
shelf

Tethys
Sea

Deep
ocean

Pangaea

Andes

Pacific Ocean

Pangaea

Desert

Forest

EXAMPLES OF TRIASSIC ANIMALS

AN EXTINCT AMPHIBIAN

A NAUTILOID MOLLUSK
(*Nautilus* sp.)

AN EXTINCT CHONDROSTEAN FISH
(*Cleithrolepis granulatus*)

AN EXTINCT NOTHOSAURIAN REPTILE
(*Pachypleurosaurus* sp.)

AN EXTINCT RHYNCHOSAURIAN REPTILE
(*Scaphonyx fischeri*)

PISANOSAURUS
A primitive ornithischian
Length: 3 ft (90 cm)

HERRERASAURUS
A herrerasaurid
Length: 10 ft (3 m)

MUSSAURUS
A plateosaurid
Length: 6 ft 6 in–10 ft (2–3 m)

MELANOROSAURUS
A melanorosaurid
Length: 40 ft (12.2 m)

Jurassic period

THE JURASSIC PERIOD, the middle part of the Mesozoic era, lasted from 208 to 144 million years ago. During the Jurassic, the landmass of Pangaea broke up into the continents of Gondwanaland and Laurasia, and sea levels rose, flooding areas of lower land. The Jurassic climate was warm and moist. Plants such as ginkgos, horsetails, and conifers thrived, and giant redwood trees appeared, as did the first flowering plants. The abundance of plant food led to the proliferation of herbivorous (plant-eating) dinosaurs, such as the large sauropods (e.g., *Diplodocus*) and stegosaurs (e.g., *Stegosaurus*). Carnivorous (flesh-eating) dinosaurs, such as *Compsognathus* and *Allosaurus*, also flourished by hunting the many animals, including other dinosaurs, that existed. Other Jurassic animals included shrewlike mammals, and pterosaurs (flying reptiles), as well as plesiosaurs and ichthyosaurs (both marine reptiles).

JURASSIC POSITIONS OF PRESENT-DAY LANDMASSES

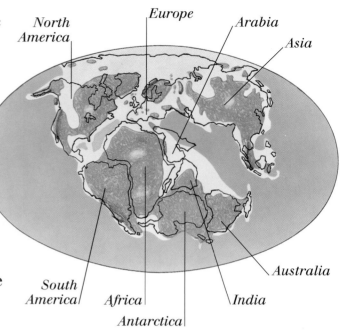

North America

Europe

Arabia

Asia

South America

Africa

Antarctica

India

Australia

EXAMPLES OF JURASSIC PLANT GROUPS

A PRESENT-DAY FERN
(Dicksonia antarctica)

A PRESENT-DAY HORSETAIL
(Equisetum arvense)

A PRESENT-DAY CONIFER
(Taxus baccata)

AN EXTINCT CONIFER

AN EXTINCT REDWOOD
(Sequoiadendron sp.)

EXAMPLES OF JURASSIC DINOSAURS

STEGOSAURUS
A stegosaurid
Length: 30 ft (9.1 m)

SCELIDOSAURUS
A scelidosaurid
Length: 13 ft (4 m)

ALLOSAURUS
An allosaurid
Length: 36 ft (11 m)

THE EARTH DURING THE JURASSIC PERIOD

Laurasia

Laurasia

North Atlantic Ocean

North American Cordillera

Ural Mountains

Turgai Strait

Forest

Laurasia

Desert

Tethys Sea

Deep ocean

Continental shelf

Forest

Desert

Andes

Gondwanaland

Pacific Ocean

Gondwanaland

EXAMPLES OF JURASSIC ANIMALS

AN EXTINCT PTEROSAUR
(*Rhamphorhynchus* sp.)

AN EXTINCT BELEMNITE MOLLUSK
(*Belemnoteuthis* sp.)

AN EXTINCT RHYNCHOSAURIAN REPTILE
(*Homeosaurus pulchellus*)

AN EXTINCT PLESIOSAUR
(*Peloneustes philarcus*)

AN EXTINCT ICHTHYOSAUR
(*Ichthyosaurus megacephalus*)

DRYOSAURUS
A dryosaurid
Length: 10–13 ft (3–4 m)

CAMPTOSAURUS
A camptosaurid
Length: 16–23 ft (4.9–7 m)

DIPLODOCUS
A diplodocid
Length: 88 ft (26.8 m)

Cretaceous period

CRETACEOUS 144-65 MYA	
JURASSIC 208-144 MYA	MESOZOIC ERA
TRIASSIC 248-208 MYA	

THE MESOZOIC ERA ENDED WITH the Cretaceous period, which lasted from 144 to 65 million years ago. During this period, Gondwanaland and Laurasia were breaking up into smaller landmasses that more closely resembled those of the modern continents. The climate remained mild and moist, but the seasons became more marked. Flowering plants, including deciduous trees, replaced many cycads, seed ferns, and conifers. Animal species became more varied, with the evolution of new mammals, insects, fish, crustaceans, and turtles. Dinosaurs evolved into a wide variety of species during the Cretaceous; more than half of all known dinosaurs – including *Iguanodon*, *Deinonychus*, *Tyrannosaurus*, and *Hypsilophodon* – lived during this period. At the end of the Cretaceous, however, large dinosaurs became extinct. The reason for this mass extinction is unknown but it is thought to have been caused by climatic changes due to either a catastrophic meteor impact with the Earth or extensive volcanic eruptions.

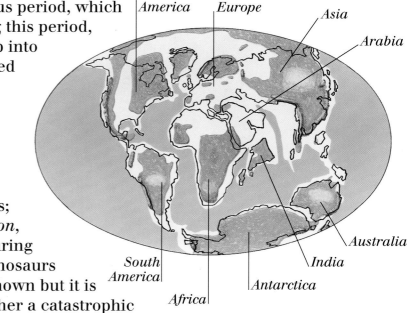

North America Europe Asia Arabia Australia India Antarctica Africa South America

EXAMPLES OF CRETACEOUS PLANT GROUPS

A PRESENT-DAY CONIFER
(*Pinus muricata*)

A PRESENT-DAY DECIDUOUS TREE
(*Magnolia* sp.)

AN EXTINCT FERN
(*Sphenopteris latiloba*)

AN EXTINCT GINKGO
(*Ginkgo pluripartita*)

AN EXTINCT DECIDUOUS TREE
(*Cercidyphyllum* sp.)

EXAMPLES OF CRETACEOUS DINOSAURS

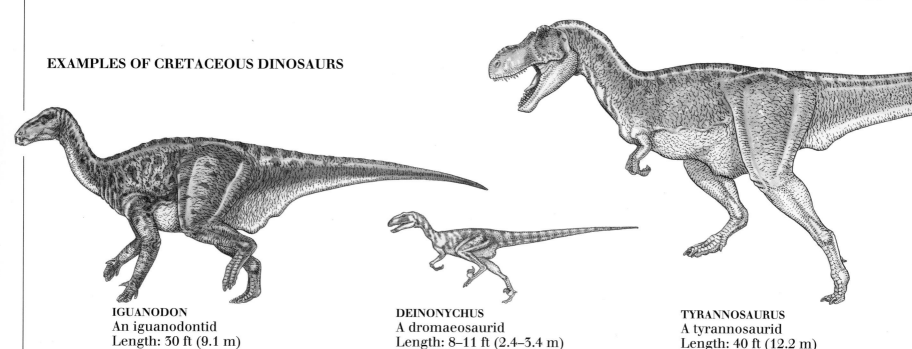

IGUANODON
An iguanodontid
Length: 30 ft (9.1 m)

DEINONYCHUS
A dromaeosaurid
Length: 8–11 ft (2.4–3.4 m)

TYRANNOSAURUS
A tyrannosaurid
Length: 40 ft (12.2 m)

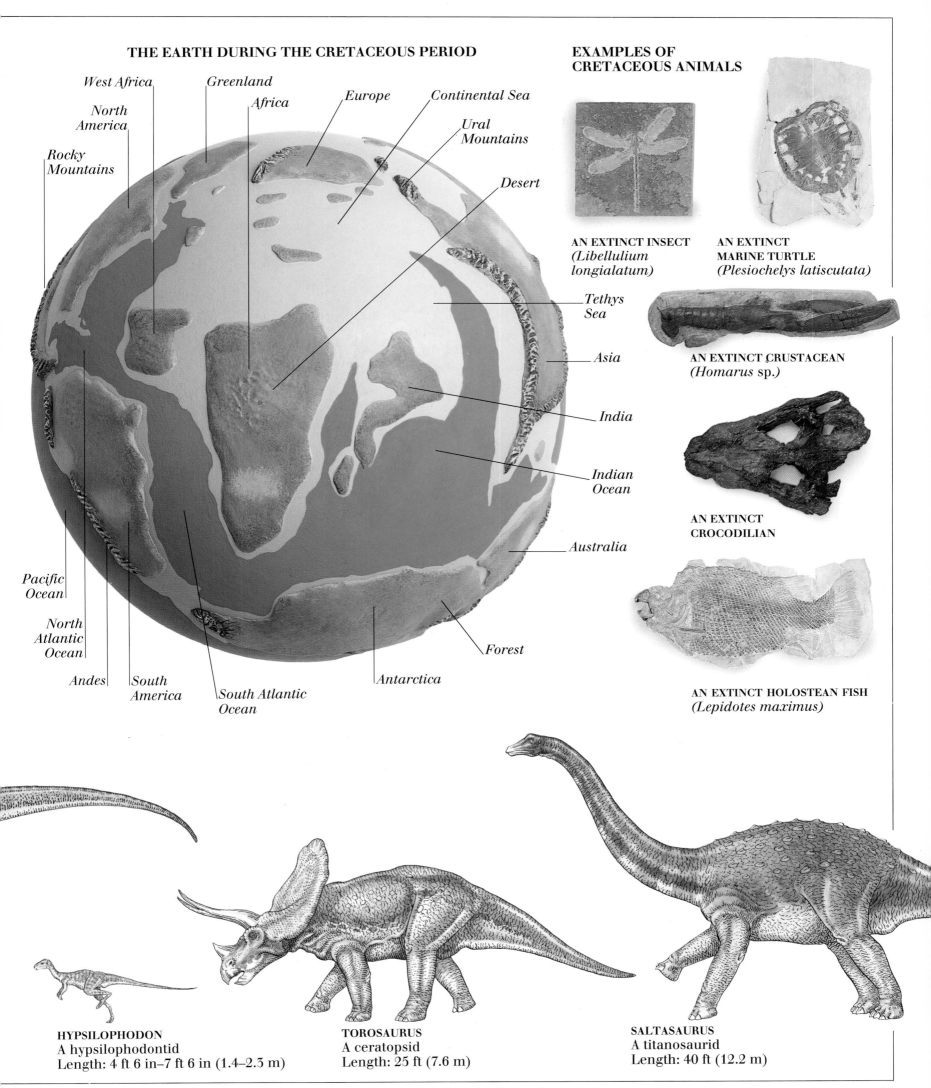

THE EARTH DURING THE CRETACEOUS PERIOD

West Africa

Greenland

Africa

Europe

Continental Sea

North America

Ural Mountains

Rocky Mountains

Desert

Tethys Sea

Asia

India

Indian Ocean

Australia

Pacific Ocean

North Atlantic Ocean

Forest

Andes

South America

South Atlantic Ocean

Antarctica

EXAMPLES OF CRETACEOUS ANIMALS

AN EXTINCT INSECT
(*Libellulium longialatum*)

AN EXTINCT MARINE TURTLE
(*Plesiochelys latiscutata*)

AN EXTINCT CRUSTACEAN
(*Homarus sp.*)

AN EXTINCT CROCODILIAN

AN EXTINCT HOLOSTEAN FISH
(*Lepidotes maximus*)

HYPSILOPHODON
A hypsilophodontid
Length: 4 ft 6 in–7 ft 6 in (1.4–2.3 m)

TOROSAURUS
A ceratopsid
Length: 25 ft (7.6 m)

SALTASAURUS
A titanosaurid
Length: 40 ft (12.2 m)

Small theropods

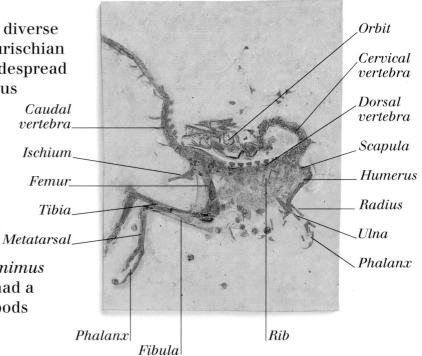

SMALL THEROPODS were a diverse group of lightweight, predatory, saurischian (lizard-hipped) dinosaurs that were widespread from Late Triassic to Late Cretaceous times (231–65 million years ago).

PROCOMPSOGNATHUS

This group included some of the smallest dinosaurs known; *Compsognathus* was one of the smallest, at about 28 in (70 cm) long, and even the largest small theropod, *Coelophysis*, was only 10 ft (3 m) long. Typical small theropods – for example, *Coelophysis*, *Ornitholestes*, and *Compsognathus* – had narrow jaws with sharp teeth; long, flexible necks; long tails; and long legs that enabled them to run fast. *Avimimus* was different from other small theropods because it had a toothless beak that resembled that of toothless theropods (see pp. 18-19).

Orbit

Cervical vertebra

Dorsal vertebra

Caudal vertebra

Ischium

Scapula

Femur

Humerus

Tibia

Radius

Metatarsal

Ulna

Phalanx

Phalanx

Rib

Fibula

EXTERNAL FEATURES OF COMPSOGNATHUS

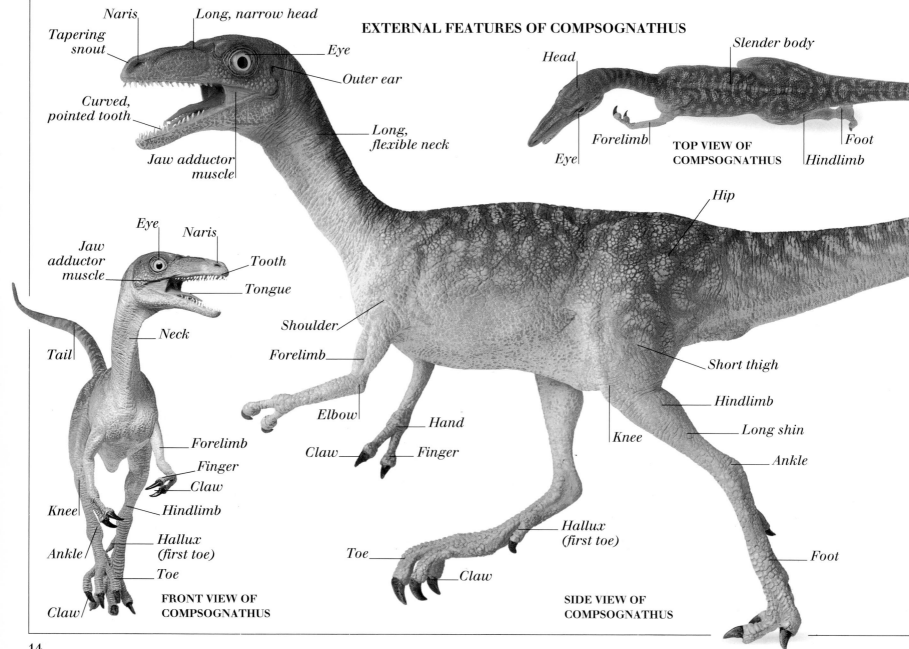

Naris

Long, narrow head

Tapering snout

Eye

Outer ear

Curved, pointed tooth

Long, flexible neck

Jaw adductor muscle

Head

Slender body

Eye

Forelimb

Foot

TOP VIEW OF COMPSOGNATHUS

Hindlimb

Hip

Eye

Naris

Jaw adductor muscle

Tooth

Tongue

Neck

Shoulder

Tail

Forelimb

Short thigh

Elbow

Hand

Hindlimb

Claw

Finger

Long shin

Forelimb

Knee

Finger

Ankle

Claw

Knee

Hallux (first toe)

Ankle

Hallux (first toe)

Toe

Toe

Foot

Claw

Claw

FRONT VIEW OF COMPSOGNATHUS

SIDE VIEW OF COMPSOGNATHUS

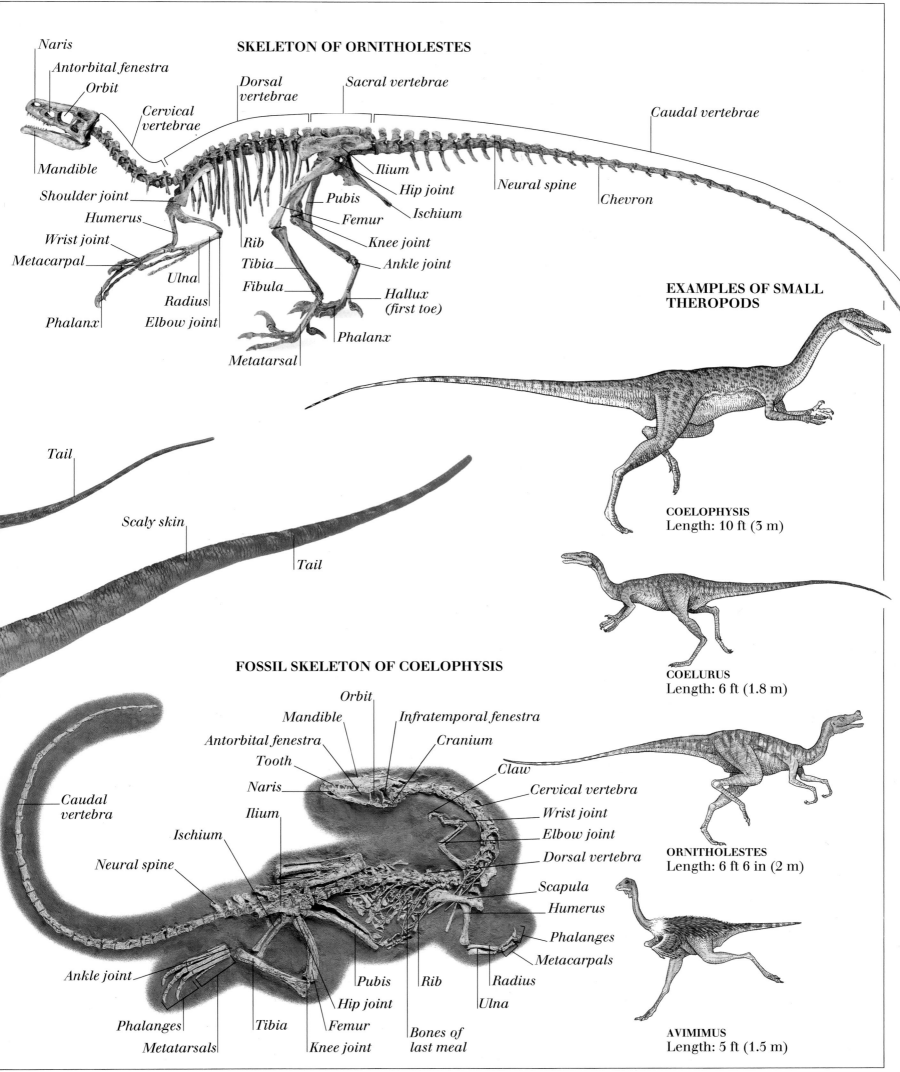

SKELETON OF ORNITHOLESTES

Naris
Antorbital fenestra
Orbit
Cervical vertebrae
Dorsal vertebrae
Sacral vertebrae
Caudal vertebrae
Mandible
Shoulder joint
Humerus
Ilium
Hip joint
Neural spine
Chevron
Pubis
Ischium
Femur
Wrist joint
Metacarpal
Rib
Knee joint
Tibia
Ankle joint
Ulna
Fibula
Hallux (first toe)
Radius
Phalanx
Elbow joint
Phalanx
Metatarsal

Tail
Scaly skin
Tail

EXAMPLES OF SMALL THEROPODS

COELOPHYSIS
Length: 10 ft (3 m)

COELURUS
Length: 6 ft (1.8 m)

ORNITHOLESTES
Length: 6 ft 6 in (2 m)

AVIMIMUS
Length: 5 ft (1.5 m)

FOSSIL SKELETON OF COELOPHYSIS

Orbit
Mandible
Infratemporal fenestra
Antorbital fenestra
Cranium
Tooth
Claw
Naris
Cervical vertebra
Ilium
Wrist joint
Caudal vertebra
Elbow joint
Ischium
Dorsal vertebra
Neural spine
Scapula
Humerus
Phalanges
Metacarpals
Ankle joint
Radius
Phalanges
Pubis
Rib
Ulna
Tibia
Hip joint
Metatarsals
Femur
Bones of last meal
Knee joint

15

Deinonychosaurs

DEINONYCHOSAURS WERE A GROUP of ferocious, predatory, saurischian (lizard-hipped) dinosaurs that lived in northern continents during the Cretaceous period (144–65 million years ago). The characteristic feature of these dinosaurs is a large, sickle-shaped claw on their second toe (deinonychosaur means "terrible claw lizard"). This claw flicked forward to slash prey during an attack. Deinonychosaurs were relatively small – ranging from about 6 ft (1.8 m) to 13 ft (4 m) in length – and agile, running on their powerful hindlegs and using their long, stiff tail to keep balance and also to help change direction quickly by acting as a rudder. It was thought that deinonychosaurs comprised two main subgroups – dromaeosaurids, such as *Deinonychus* and *Dromaeosaurus*, and troodontids, such as *Troodon* – but recent evidence suggests that dromaeosaurids and troodontids are not as closely related as previously believed. Dromaeosaurids had eyes at the side of the head, giving them a wide angle of vision. Their "terrible claws" were large. By hunting in packs, dromaeosaurids may have brought down prey much larger than themselves. By contrast, troodontids had smaller "terrible claws" and large, forward-facing eyes, which may have given them three-dimensional vision. Troodontids had larger brains, relative to their body size, than those of any other known dinosaur.

"Terrible claw" in resting position

Metatarsal

"Terrible claw"

Arc of claw movement

Enlarged joint

Phalanx

"Terrible claw" in flexed position

Claw

MOVEMENT OF "TERRIBLE CLAW"

SKELETON OF FOOT

SKELETON OF DROMAEOSAURUS

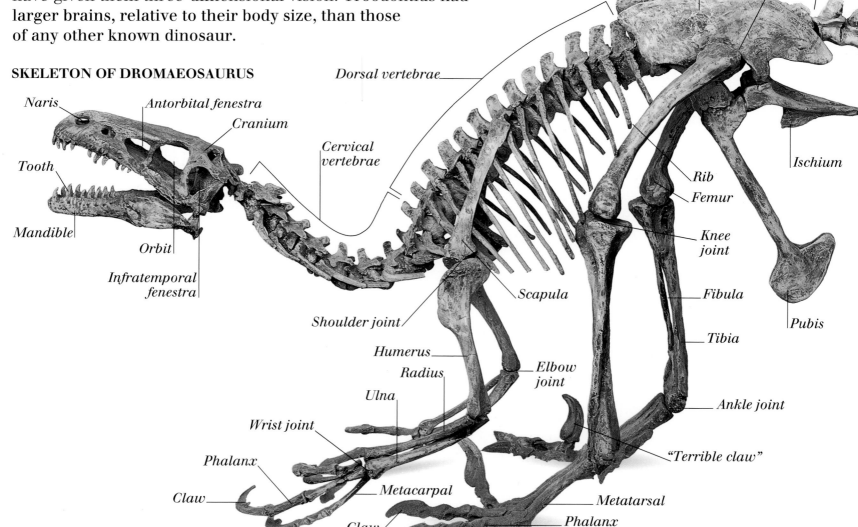

Naris

Antorbital fenestra

Cranium

Dorsal vertebrae

Ilium

Hip joint

Cervical vertebrae

Tooth

Mandible

Orbit

Infratemporal fenestra

Scapula

Shoulder joint

Humerus

Radius

Ulna

Wrist joint

Phalanx

Claw

Metacarpal

Claw

Elbow joint

Rib

Femur

Knee joint

Fibula

Tibia

Ischium

Pubis

Ankle joint

"Terrible claw"

Metatarsal

Phalanx

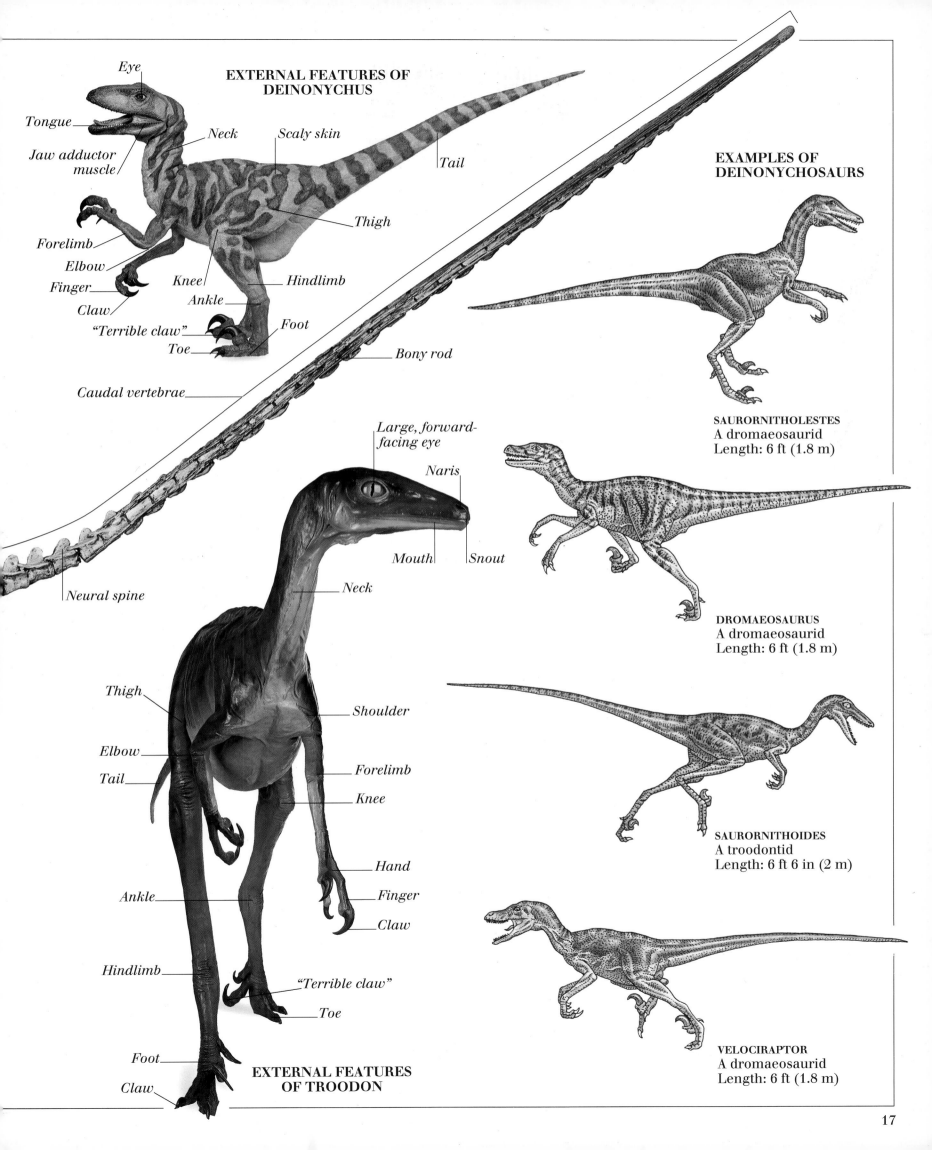

EXTERNAL FEATURES OF DEINONYCHUS

Eye

Tongue

Jaw adductor muscle

Neck

Scaly skin

Tail

Forelimb

Elbow

Thigh

Finger

Knee

Hindlimb

Claw

Ankle

"Terrible claw"

Foot

Toe

Bony rod

Caudal vertebrae

Neural spine

EXAMPLES OF DEINONYCHOSAURS

SAURORNITHOLESTES
A dromaeosaurid
Length: 6 ft (1.8 m)

DROMAEOSAURUS
A dromaeosaurid
Length: 6 ft (1.8 m)

SAURORNITHOIDES
A troodontid
Length: 6 ft 6 in (2 m)

VELOCIRAPTOR
A dromaeosaurid
Length: 6 ft (1.8 m)

Large, forward-facing eye

Naris

Mouth

Snout

Neck

Thigh

Shoulder

Elbow

Forelimb

Tail

Knee

Ankle

Hand

Finger

Claw

Hindlimb

"Terrible claw"

Toe

Foot

Claw

EXTERNAL FEATURES OF TROODON

Toothless theropods

TOOTHLESS THEROPODS COMPRISED TWO MAIN SUBGROUPS OF saurischian (lizard-hipped) dinosaur: ornithomimosaurs and oviraptorosaurs. Both groups lived during Late Cretaceous times (97.5–65 million years ago) in what are now Asia, North America, and Africa. They had toothless beaks, in contrast to the small theropods (see pp. 14-15), which had jaws containing small, sharp teeth. Ornithomimosaurs (meaning "bird-mimic lizards"), such as *Gallimimus*, *Ornithomimus*, *Struthiomimus*, and *Dromiceiomimus*, had some features in common with the modern ostrich: a small head with a long, narrow beak, a long neck, and powerful hindlimbs. Oviraptorosaurs (meaning "egg-plundering lizards"), such as *Oviraptor* (see p. 32), also had ostrich-like features, but their beaks were short. The internal anatomy of ornithomimosaurs and oviraptorosaurs is thought to have resembled that of modern birds, with a gizzard (muscular stomach) for grinding up food.

Eye

Toothless beak

Cervical musculature

INTERNAL ANATOMY OF FEMALE GALLIMIMUS

Neural spine

Scapula

Lung

Gizzard

Rib

Dorsal vertebra

Ovary

Kidney

Ilium

Hip joint

Femur

Neural spine

Caudal vertebra

Trachea

Shoulder joint

Coracoid

Heart

Humerus

Posterior brachial muscle

Anterior brachial muscle

Claw

Anterior antebrachial muscle

Ulna

Metacarpal

Liver

Intestine

Posterior antebrachial muscle

Pubis

Femoral musculature

Chevron

Cloaca

Ischium

Tibia

Anterior crural muscle

Posterior crural muscle

Fibula

Tarsal

Metatarsal

Tendon

Phalanx

Antorbital fenestra

Maxilla

Naris

Mandible

Orbit

Cranium

Mandibular fenestra

SKULL AND MANDIBLE OF DROMICEIOMIMUS

Toothless beak

Neck

Scaly skin

Tail

Elbow

Hand

Ankle

Claw

Foot

EXTERNAL FEATURES OF GALLIMIMUS

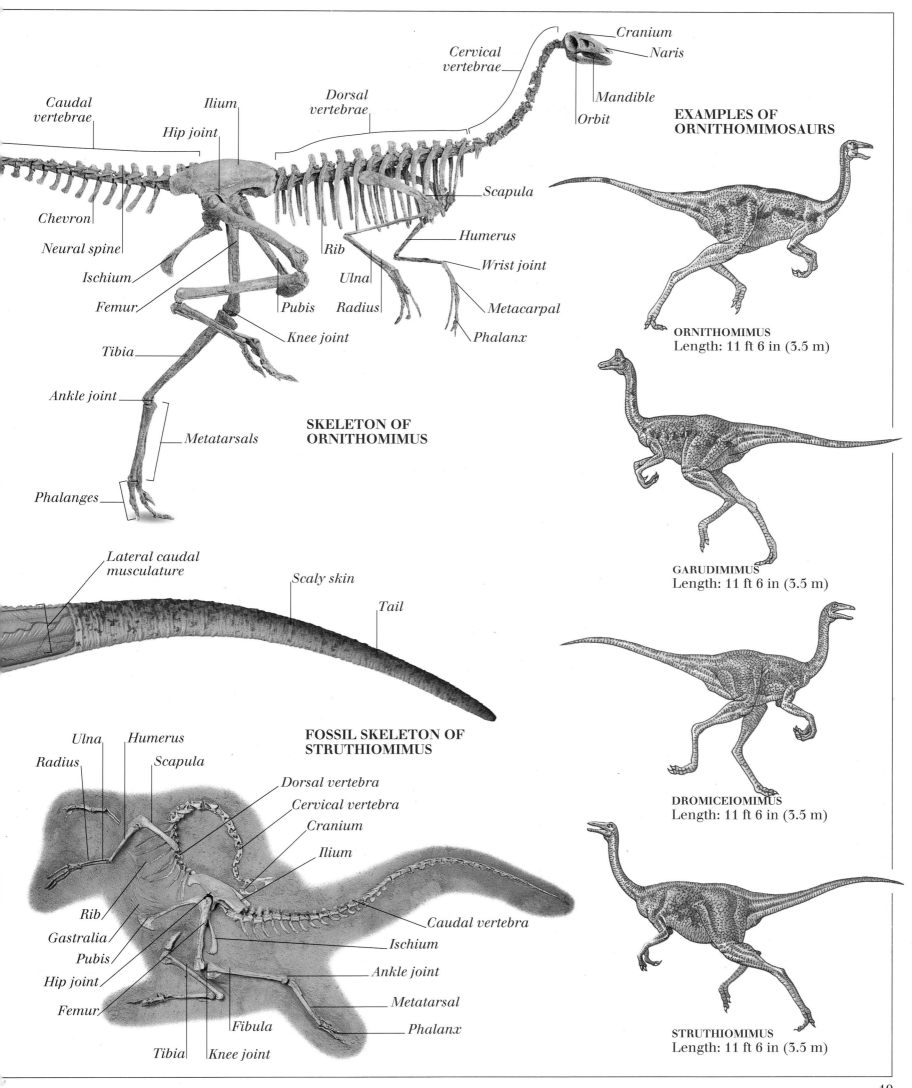

Caudal
vertebrae

Ilium

Dorsal
vertebrae

Cervical
vertebrae

Cranium

Naris

Hip joint

Mandible

Orbit

**EXAMPLES OF
ORNITHOMIMOSAURS**

Chevron

Scapula

Neural spine

Humerus

Ischium

Rib

Wrist joint

Femur

Ulna

Pubis

Radius

Metacarpal

Knee joint

Phalanx

Tibia

ORNITHOMIMUS
Length: 11 ft 6 in (3.5 m)

Ankle joint

Metatarsals

**SKELETON OF
ORNITHOMIMUS**

Phalanges

Lateral caudal
musculature

Scaly skin

Tail

GARUDIMIMUS
Length: 11 ft 6 in (3.5 m)

Ulna

Humerus

**FOSSIL SKELETON OF
STRUTHIOMIMUS**

Radius

Scapula

Dorsal vertebra

Cervical vertebra

Cranium

Ilium

DROMICEIOMIMUS
Length: 11 ft 6 in (3.5 m)

Rib

Caudal vertebra

Gastralia

Ischium

Pubis

Hip joint

Ankle joint

Femur

Metatarsal

Fibula

Phalanx

Tibia

Knee joint

STRUTHIOMIMUS
Length: 11 ft 6 in (3.5 m)

Carnosaurs 1

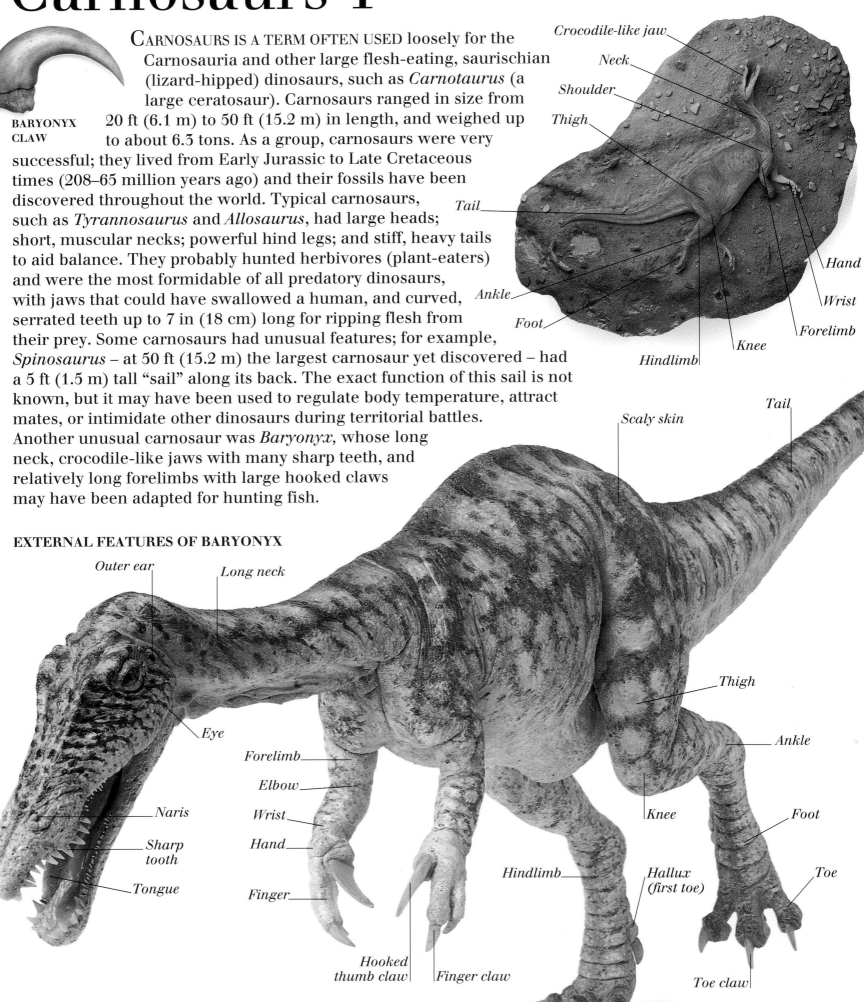

CARNOSAURS IS A TERM OFTEN USED loosely for the Carnosauria and other large flesh-eating, saurischian (lizard-hipped) dinosaurs, such as *Carnotaurus* (a large ceratosaur). Carnosaurs ranged in size from 20 ft (6.1 m) to 50 ft (15.2 m) in length, and weighed up to about 6.3 tons. As a group, carnosaurs were very successful; they lived from Early Jurassic to Late Cretaceous times (208–65 million years ago) and their fossils have been discovered throughout the world. Typical carnosaurs, such as *Tyrannosaurus* and *Allosaurus*, had large heads; short, muscular necks; powerful hind legs; and stiff, heavy tails to aid balance. They probably hunted herbivores (plant-eaters) and were the most formidable of all predatory dinosaurs, with jaws that could have swallowed a human, and curved, serrated teeth up to 7 in (18 cm) long for ripping flesh from their prey. Some carnosaurs had unusual features; for example, *Spinosaurus* – at 50 ft (15.2 m) the largest carnosaur yet discovered – had a 5 ft (1.5 m) tall "sail" along its back. The exact function of this sail is not known, but it may have been used to regulate body temperature, attract mates, or intimidate other dinosaurs during territorial battles. Another unusual carnosaur was *Baryonyx*, whose long neck, crocodile-like jaws with many sharp teeth, and relatively long forelimbs with large hooked claws may have been adapted for hunting fish.

BARYONYX
CLAW

**MODEL OF BARYONYX
IN DEATH POSITION**

Crocodile-like jaw

Neck

Shoulder

Thigh

Tail

Ankle

Foot

Hindlimb

Knee

Hand

Wrist

Forelimb

EXTERNAL FEATURES OF BARYONYX

Outer ear

Long neck

Eye

Naris

Sharp
tooth

Tongue

Forelimb

Elbow

Wrist

Hand

Finger

Hooked
thumb claw

Finger claw

Scaly skin

Tail

Thigh

Ankle

Knee

Foot

Hindlimb

Hallux
(first toe)

Toe

Toe claw

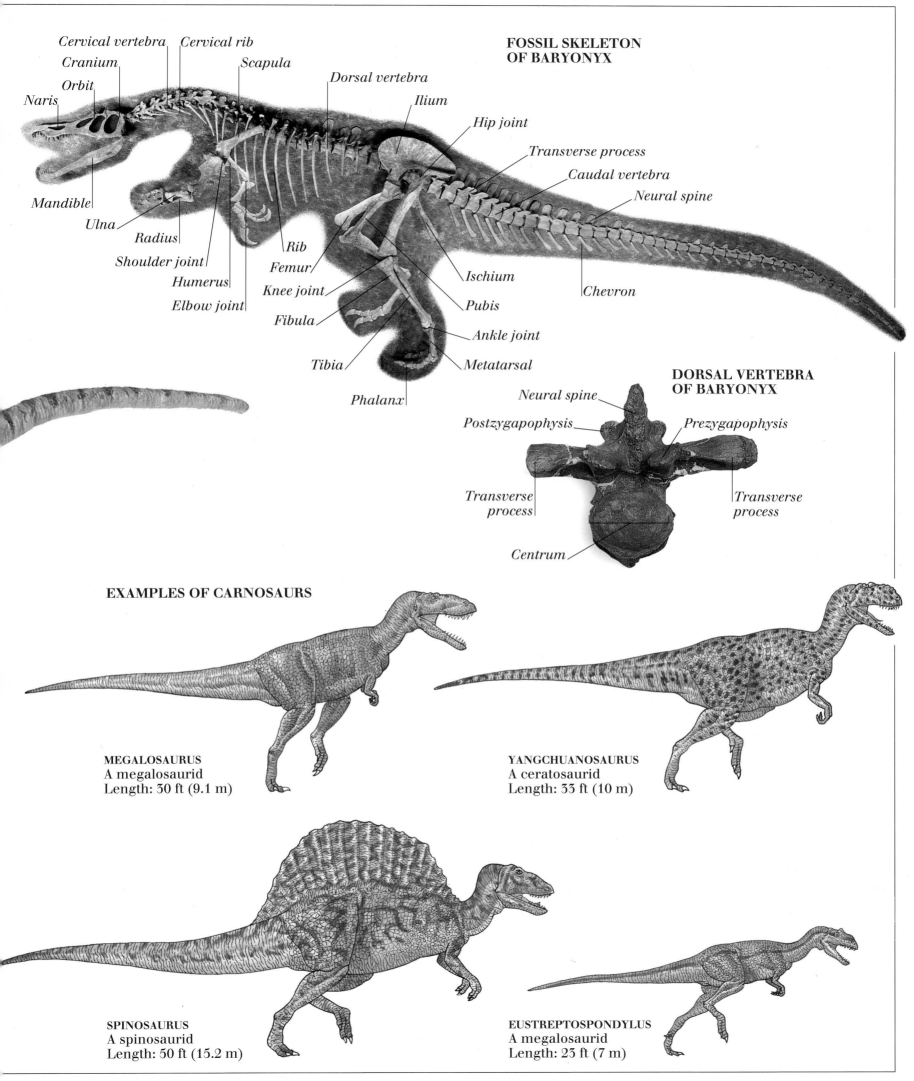

**FOSSIL SKELETON
OF BARYONYX**

Cervical vertebra

Cervical rib

Cranium

Scapula

Orbit

Dorsal vertebra

Naris

Ilium

Hip joint

Transverse process

Caudal vertebra

Neural spine

Mandible

Ulna

Radius

Rib

Shoulder joint

Femur

Humerus

Ischium

Elbow joint

Knee joint

Pubis

Chevron

Fibula

Ankle joint

Tibia

Metatarsal

Phalanx

**DORSAL VERTEBRA
OF BARYONYX**

Neural spine

Postzygapophysis

Prezygapophysis

Transverse
process

Transverse
process

Centrum

EXAMPLES OF CARNOSAURS

MEGALOSAURUS
A megalosaurid
Length: 30 ft (9.1 m)

YANGCHUANOSAURUS
A ceratosaurid
Length: 33 ft (10 m)

SPINOSAURUS
A spinosaurid
Length: 50 ft (15.2 m)

EUSTREPTOSPONDYLUS
A megalosaurid
Length: 23 ft (7 m)

Carnosaurs 2

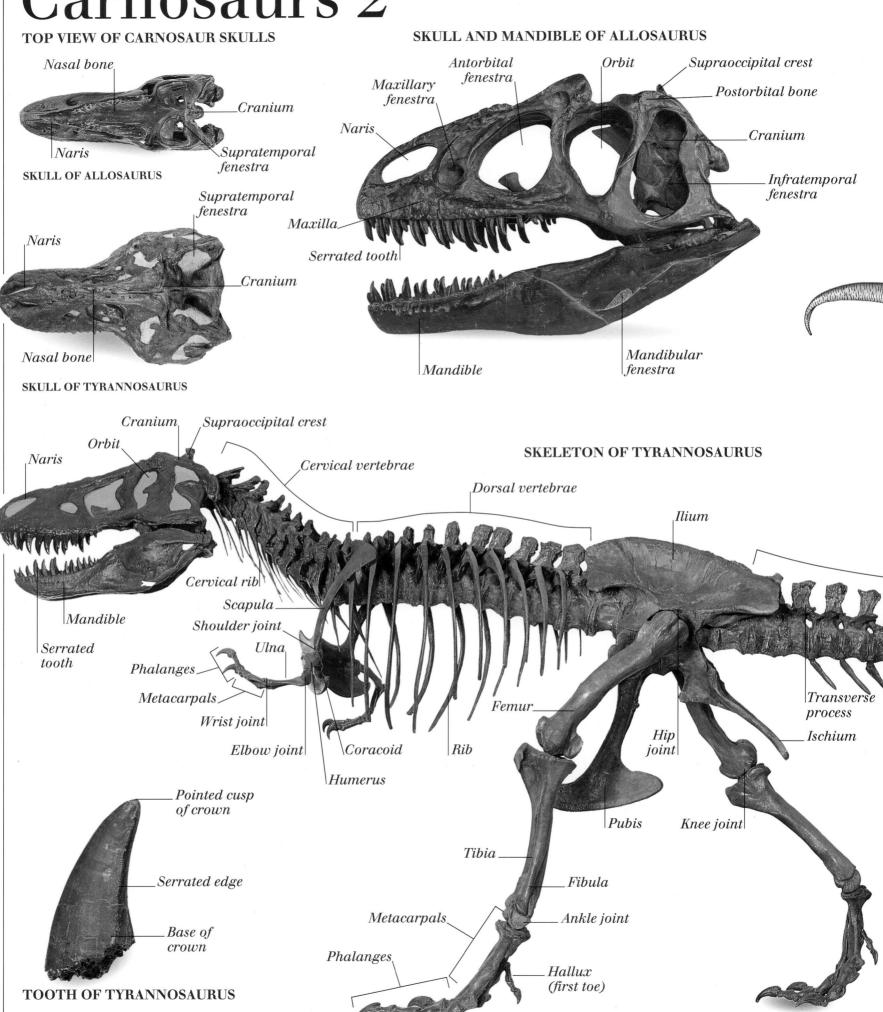

TOP VIEW OF CARNOSAUR SKULLS

Nasal bone

Cranium

Naris

Supratemporal fenestra

SKULL OF ALLOSAURUS

Supratemporal fenestra

Naris

Cranium

Nasal bone

SKULL OF TYRANNOSAURUS

SKULL AND MANDIBLE OF ALLOSAURUS

Antorbital fenestra

Orbit

Supraoccipital crest

Maxillary fenestra

Postorbital bone

Naris

Cranium

Maxilla

Infratemporal fenestra

Serrated tooth

Mandible

Mandibular fenestra

SKELETON OF TYRANNOSAURUS

Cranium

Supraoccipital crest

Orbit

Cervical vertebrae

Dorsal vertebrae

Ilium

Naris

Cervical rib

Scapula

Shoulder joint

Ulna

Phalanges

Metacarpals

Wrist joint

Transverse process

Elbow joint

Coracoid

Rib

Femur

Ischium

Humerus

Hip joint

Mandible

Serrated tooth

Pubis

Knee joint

Pointed cusp of crown

Tibia

Fibula

Serrated edge

Metacarpals

Ankle joint

Base of crown

Phalanges

Hallux (first toe)

TOOTH OF TYRANNOSAURUS

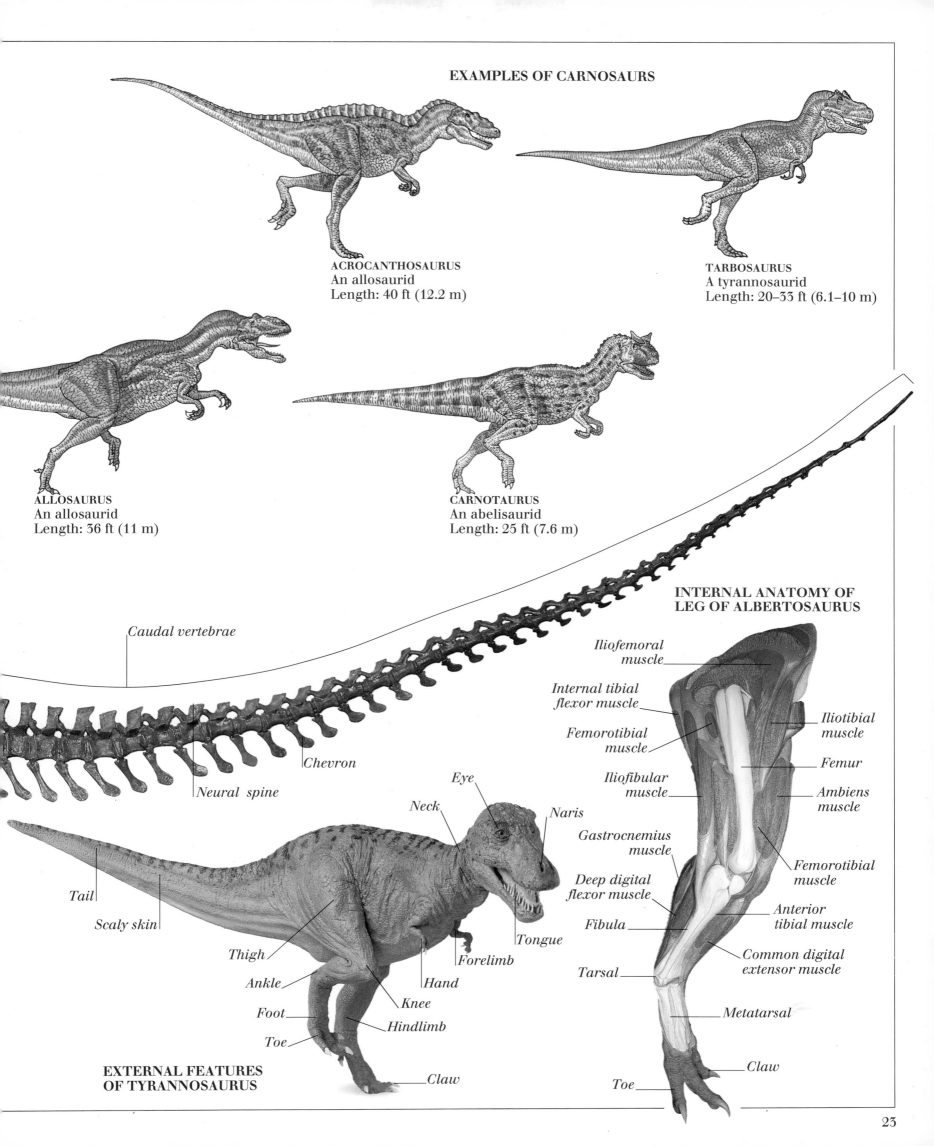

EXAMPLES OF CARNOSAURS

ACROCANTHOSAURUS
An allosaurid
Length: 40 ft (12.2 m)

TARBOSAURUS
A tyrannosaurid
Length: 20–33 ft (6.1–10 m)

ALLOSAURUS
An allosaurid
Length: 36 ft (11 m)

CARNOTAURUS
An abelisaurid
Length: 25 ft (7.6 m)

Caudal vertebrae

Chevron

Neural spine

INTERNAL ANATOMY OF LEG OF ALBERTOSAURUS

Iliofemoral muscle

Internal tibial flexor muscle

Femorotibial muscle

Iliofibular muscle

Gastrocnemius muscle

Deep digital flexor muscle

Fibula

Tarsal

Iliotibial muscle

Femur

Ambiens muscle

Femorotibial muscle

Anterior tibial muscle

Common digital extensor muscle

Metatarsal

Claw

Toe

Eye

Neck

Naris

Tongue

Forelimb

Hand

Knee

Hindlimb

Thigh

Ankle

Foot

Toe

Tail

Scaly skin

Claw

EXTERNAL FEATURES OF TYRANNOSAURUS

Prosauropods

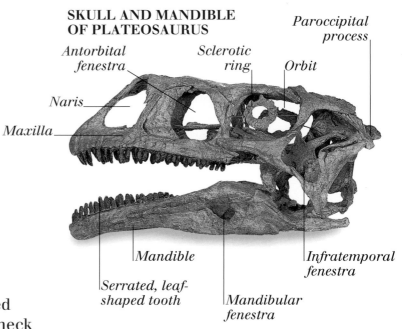

SKULL AND MANDIBLE OF PLATEOSAURUS

PROSAUROPODS WERE A group of saurischian (lizard-hipped) dinosaurs that lived from Late Triassic to Early Jurassic times (231–188 million years ago); they were distributed throughout the world. They are thought to have been the first large herbivorous (plant-eating) dinosaurs and may have had the same ancestors as sauropods (see pp. 26-29). Prosauropods varied considerably in size: *Anchisaurus* was one of the smaller prosauropods, at about 8 ft (2.4 m) long, and *Melanorosaurus* was one of the larger, at approximately 40 ft (12.2 m) long. Typical features of prosauropods included a small head containing leaf-shaped teeth, a relatively long neck and tail, and hindlimbs that were longer than the forelimbs; all known prosauropods had large, curved thumb claws.

THECODONTOSAURUS

- Antorbital fenestra
- Naris
- Maxilla
- Sclerotic ring
- Paroccipital process
- Orbit
- Mandible
- Serrated, leaf-shaped tooth
- Mandibular fenestra
- Infratemporal fenestra

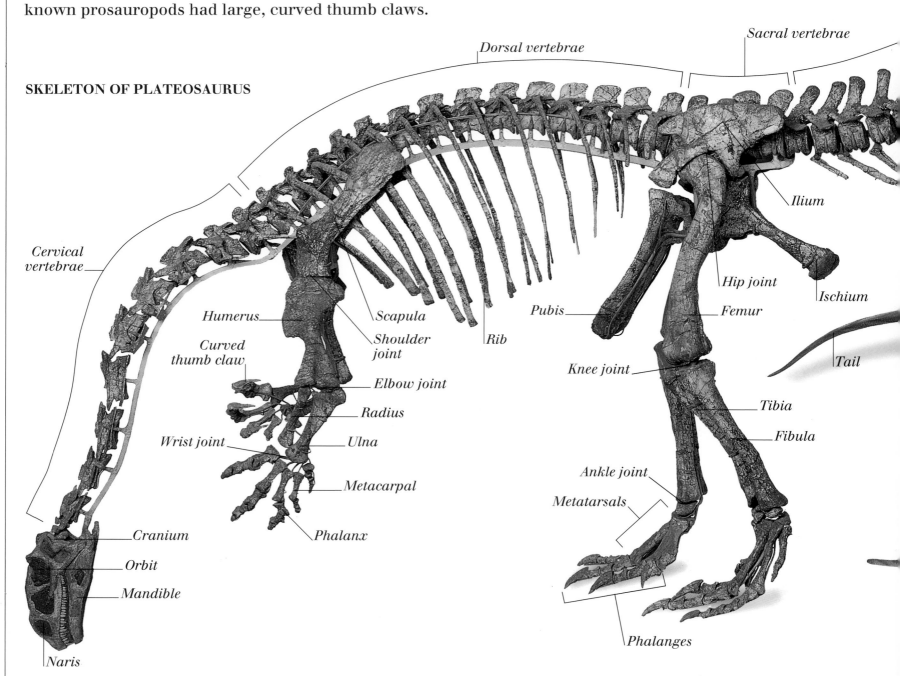

SKELETON OF PLATEOSAURUS

- Dorsal vertebrae
- Sacral vertebrae
- Cervical vertebrae
- Ilium
- Hip joint
- Ischium
- Humerus
- Curved thumb claw
- Scapula
- Shoulder joint
- Rib
- Pubis
- Femur
- Tail
- Knee joint
- Elbow joint
- Radius
- Wrist joint
- Ulna
- Tibia
- Fibula
- Metacarpal
- Ankle joint
- Metatarsals
- Cranium
- Phalanx
- Orbit
- Mandible
- Phalanges
- Naris

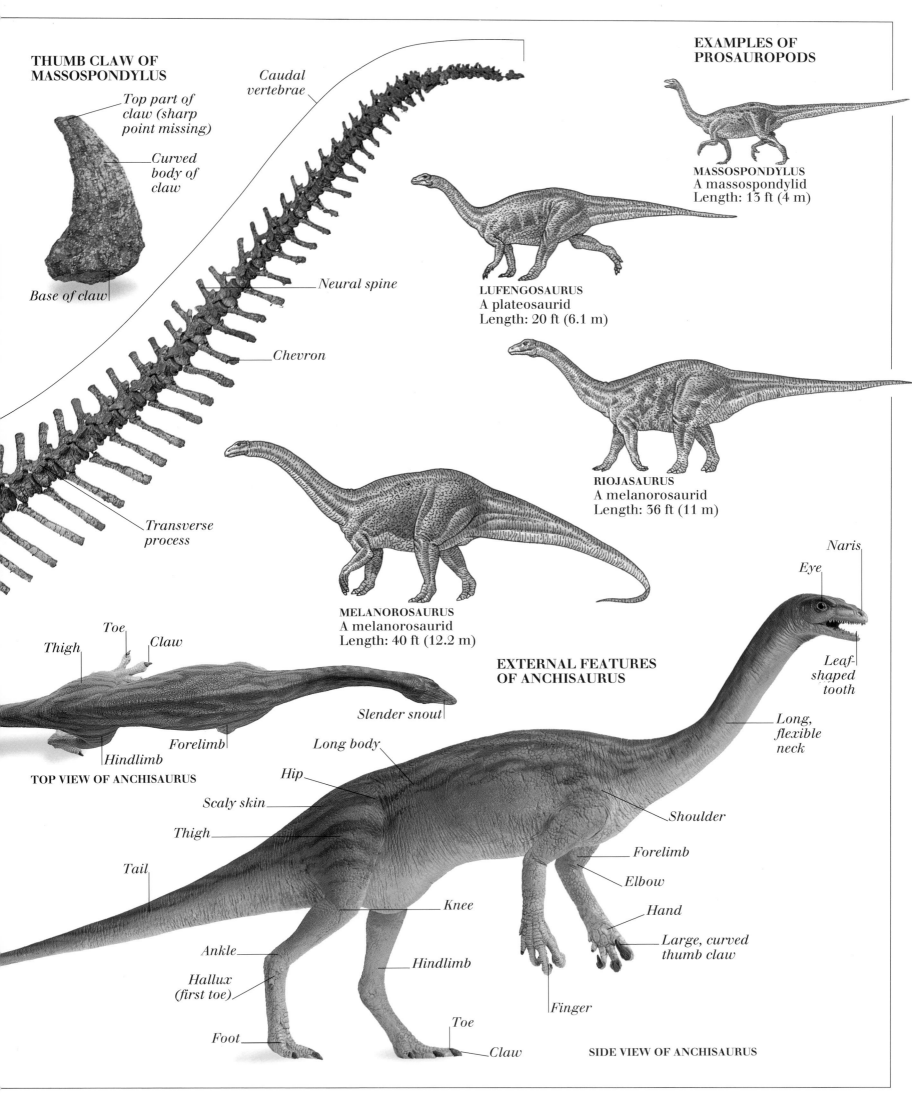

THUMB CLAW OF MASSOSPONDYLUS

Top part of claw (sharp point missing)

Curved body of claw

Base of claw

Caudal vertebrae

Neural spine

Chevron

Transverse process

MASSOSPONDYLUS
A massospondylid
Length: 13 ft (4 m)

LUFENGOSAURUS
A plateosaurid
Length: 20 ft (6.1 m)

RIOJASAURUS
A melanorosaurid
Length: 36 ft (11 m)

MELANOROSAURUS
A melanorosaurid
Length: 40 ft (12.2 m)

Thigh

Toe

Claw

Slender snout

Forelimb

Hindlimb

TOP VIEW OF ANCHISAURUS

EXTERNAL FEATURES OF ANCHISAURUS

Naris

Eye

Leaf-shaped tooth

Long, flexible neck

Long body

Hip

Scaly skin

Thigh

Shoulder

Forelimb

Elbow

Hand

Tail

Knee

Large, curved thumb claw

Ankle

Hindlimb

Hallux (first toe)

Finger

Foot

Toe

Claw

SIDE VIEW OF ANCHISAURUS

SAUROPODS FORMED A large group of saurischian (lizard-hipped) dinosaurs that included some of the largest animals ever to have lived. *Brachiosaurus* was one of the heaviest, weighing up to 77 tons, which is more than the weight of 10 elephants.

GASTROLITHS (GIZZARD STONES)

Diplodocus was one of the longest sauropods; measuring about 90 ft (27.4 m) from head to tail, it was almost as long as a blue whale, which, at about 100 ft (30.5 m), is the longest living animal. Sauropods supported their massive weight on pillar-like legs, which probably resembled those of elephants (see p. 28). As a group, sauropods were among the most successful dinosaurs: they were found throughout the world from Early Jurassic to Late Cretaceous times (208–65 million years ago). As well as being huge, sauropods typically had small heads; long, flexible necks; bulky bodies; and long tails. Some sauropods' bones were honeycombed with pleurocoels (hollows) to minimize weight. Sauropods were herbivores and, being so large, needed to eat vast amounts of vegetation. Consequently, their long necks – up to 49 ft (14.9 m) long in the case of *Mamenchisaurus* – were a great advantage, enabling them to reach vegetation that was too high up for other dinosaurs. Sauropods had no grinding teeth, which suggests that they swallowed food without chewing it; instead, food was probably ground up by gastroliths (stones) in the gizzard (muscular stomach).

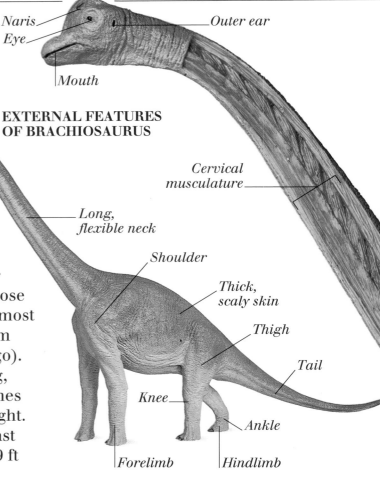

EXTERNAL FEATURES OF BRACHIOSAURUS

Naris
Eye
Outer ear
Mouth
Snout
Eye
Cervical musculature
Long, flexible neck
Shoulder
Thick, scaly skin
Thigh
Tail
Knee
Ankle
Forelimb
Hindlimb

EXAMPLES OF SAUROPOD SKULLS

Antorbital fenestra
Maxillary fenestra
Maxilla
Orbit
Cranium
Peg-shaped tooth
Sclerotic ring
Infratemporal fenestra
Mandible

SKULL AND MANDIBLE OF DIPLODOCUS

FOSSIL EGGS OF TITANOSAURID

Fossil eggshell fragment
Fossil egg
Fossil eggshell fragment

Orbit
Naris
Cranium
Antorbital fenestra
Infratemporal fenestra
Maxilla
Mandible
Spoon-shaped tooth

SKULL AND MANDIBLE OF CAMARASAURUS

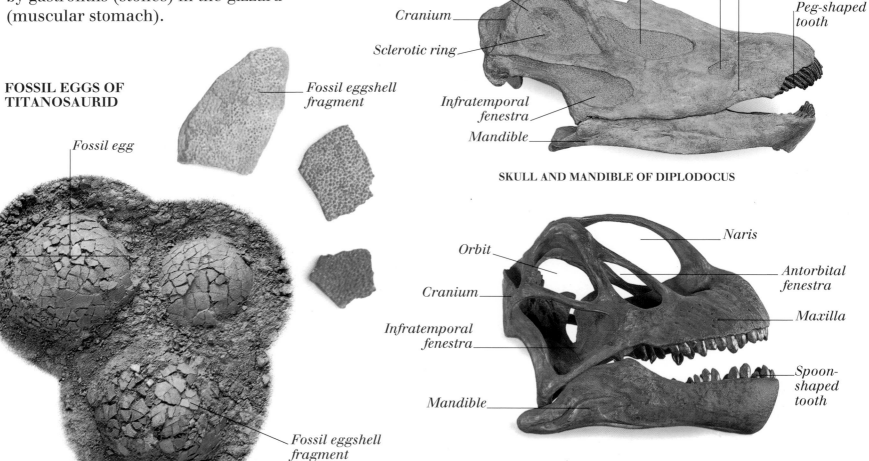

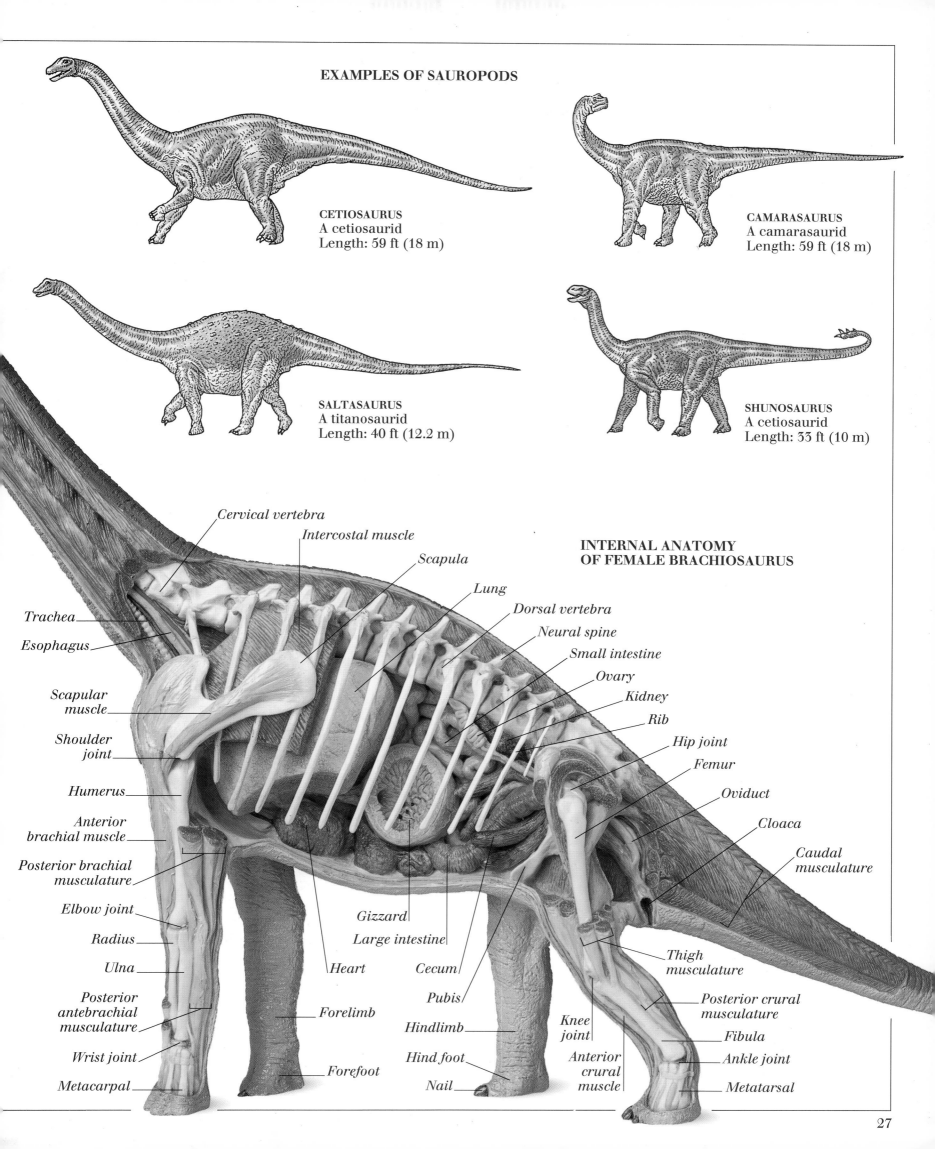

EXAMPLES OF SAUROPODS

CETIOSAURUS
A cetiosaurid
Length: 59 ft (18 m)

CAMARASAURUS
A camarasaurid
Length: 59 ft (18 m)

SALTASAURUS
A titanosaurid
Length: 40 ft (12.2 m)

SHUNOSAURUS
A cetiosaurid
Length: 33 ft (10 m)

INTERNAL ANATOMY
OF FEMALE BRACHIOSAURUS

Cervical vertebra

Intercostal muscle

Scapula

Lung

Dorsal vertebra

Neural spine

Small intestine

Ovary

Kidney

Rib

Hip joint

Femur

Oviduct

Cloaca

Caudal musculature

Trachea

Esophagus

Scapular muscle

Shoulder joint

Humerus

Anterior brachial muscle

Posterior brachial musculature

Elbow joint

Radius

Ulna

Posterior antebrachial musculature

Wrist joint

Metacarpal

Forelimb

Forefoot

Gizzard

Large intestine

Heart

Cecum

Pubis

Hindlimb

Hind foot

Nail

Knee joint

Anterior crural muscle

Thigh musculature

Posterior crural musculature

Fibula

Ankle joint

Metatarsal

Sauropods 2

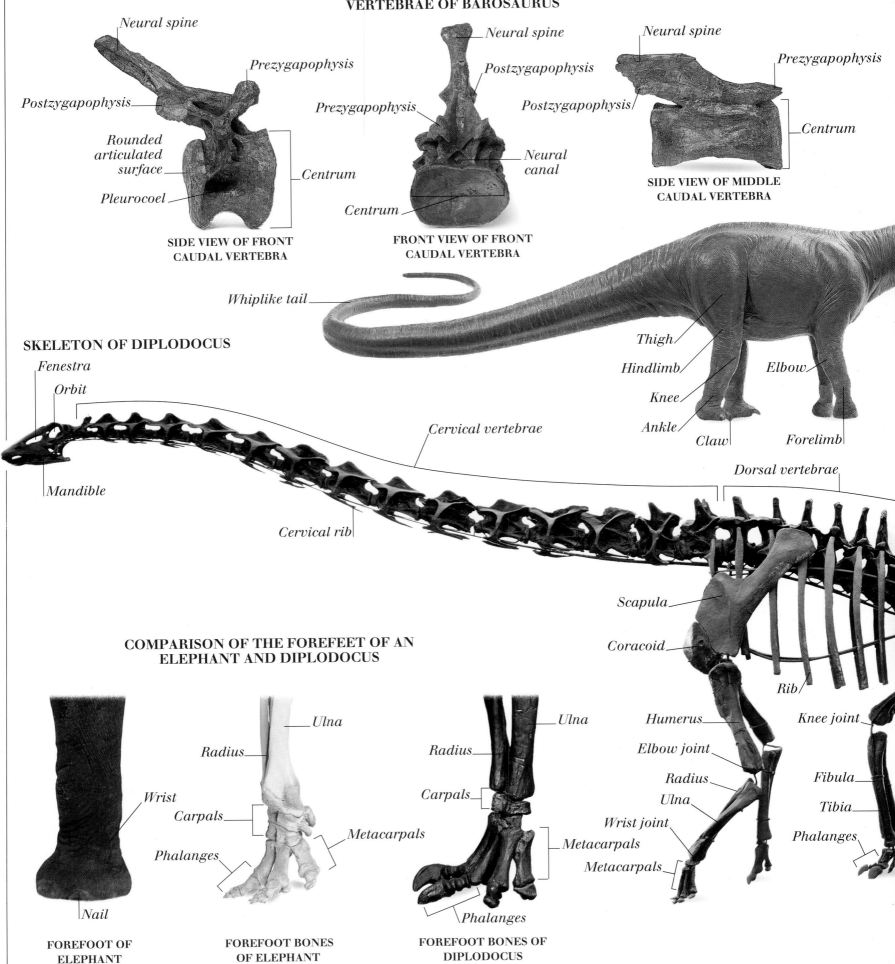

Neural spine

Prezygapophysis

Postzygapophysis

Rounded
articulated
surface

Centrum

Pleurocoel

**SIDE VIEW OF FRONT
CAUDAL VERTEBRA**

Neural spine

Postzygapophysis

Prezygapophysis

Neural
canal

Centrum

**FRONT VIEW OF FRONT
CAUDAL VERTEBRA**

Neural spine

Prezygapophysis

Postzygapophysis

Centrum

**SIDE VIEW OF MIDDLE
CAUDAL VERTEBRA**

Whiplike tail

Thigh

Hindlimb

Knee

Ankle

Claw

Elbow

Forelimb

SKELETON OF DIPLODOCUS

Fenestra

Orbit

Mandible

Cervical rib

Cervical vertebrae

Dorsal vertebrae

Scapula

Coracoid

Rib

Humerus

Elbow joint

Radius

Ulna

Wrist joint

Metacarpals

Metacarpals

Knee joint

Fibula

Tibia

Phalanges

**COMPARISON OF THE FOREFEET OF AN
ELEPHANT AND DIPLODOCUS**

Wrist

Nail

**FOREFOOT OF
ELEPHANT**

Ulna

Radius

Carpals

Metacarpals

Phalanges

**FOREFOOT BONES
OF ELEPHANT**

Ulna

Radius

Carpals

Metacarpals

Phalanges

**FOREFOOT BONES OF
DIPLODOCUS**

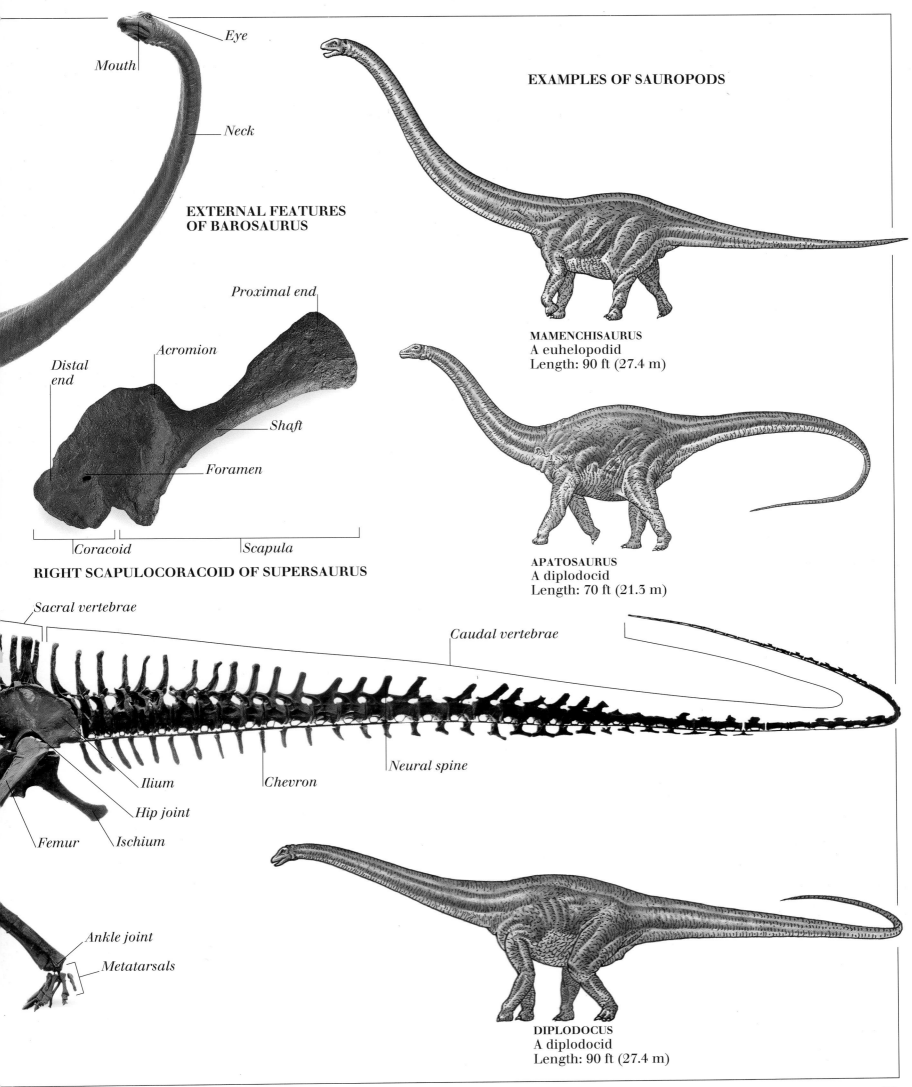

Eye

Mouth

Neck

**EXTERNAL FEATURES
OF BAROSAURUS**

EXAMPLES OF SAUROPODS

Proximal end

Acromion

Distal
end

Shaft

Foramen

Coracoid

Scapula

RIGHT SCAPULOCORACOID OF SUPERSAURUS

MAMENCHISAURUS
A euhelopodid
Length: 90 ft (27.4 m)

APATOSAURUS
A diplodocid
Length: 70 ft (21.3 m)

Sacral vertebrae

Caudal vertebrae

Neural spine

Ilium

Chevron

Hip joint

Femur

Ischium

Ankle joint

Metatarsals

DIPLODOCUS
A diplodocid
Length: 90 ft (27.4 m)

29

Herbivores' heads

HERBIVOROUS (PLANT-EATING) DINOSAURS probably spent much of their time eating. The wide range of vegetation consumed by the various herbivores may be reflected in the diversity of their heads, particularly of their jaws and teeth. For example, *Gallimimus* had a beak, possibly for cropping fruit and vegetation, *Anchisaurus* had ridged teeth for shredding the leaves from plants, *Stegosaurus* had a beak, and cheek teeth for grinding vegetation, and *Triceratops* had batteries of cheek teeth for slicing up plant food. The jaws of some herbivorous dinosaurs could move from side to side, which enabled them to grind up vegetation in their mouths. Other herbivores relied on gastroliths (stones) in their gizzard (muscular stomach) to break up the vegetation they had eaten. Most herbivorous dinosaurs had eyes at the sides of their heads, giving them a wide angle of vision so that they could spot predators approaching from any direction. Some herbivores had distinctive features on their heads. For example, *Triceratops* had massive brow horns, possibly for use in territorial battles, and hadrosaurs, such as *Brachylophosaurus*, had crests that distinguished one species from another within a herd.

SAUROPOD TEETH

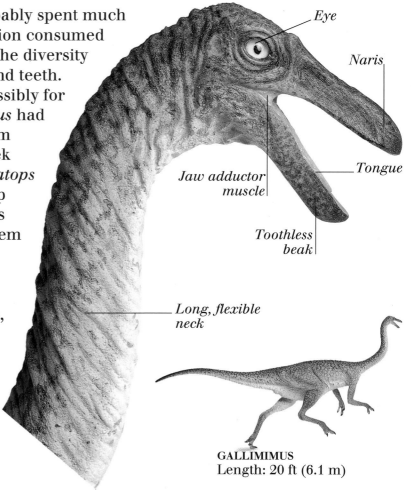

Eye

Naris

Tongue

Jaw adductor muscle

Toothless beak

Long, flexible neck

GALLIMIMUS
Length: 20 ft (6.1 m)

HEAD OF STEGOSAURUS

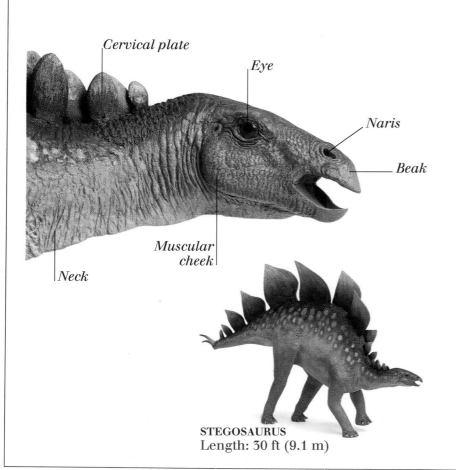

Cervical plate

Eye

Naris

Beak

Muscular cheek

Neck

STEGOSAURUS
Length: 30 ft (9.1 m)

HEAD OF ANCHISAURUS

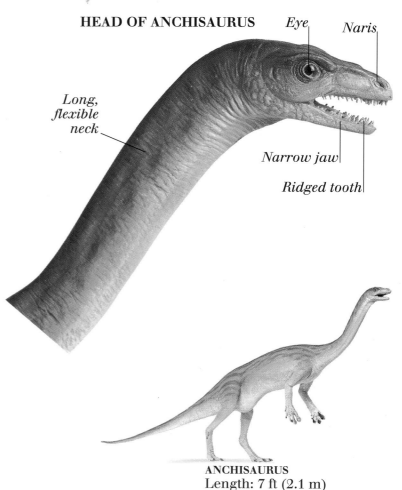

Eye

Naris

Long, flexible neck

Narrow jaw

Ridged tooth

ANCHISAURUS
Length: 7 ft (2.1 m)

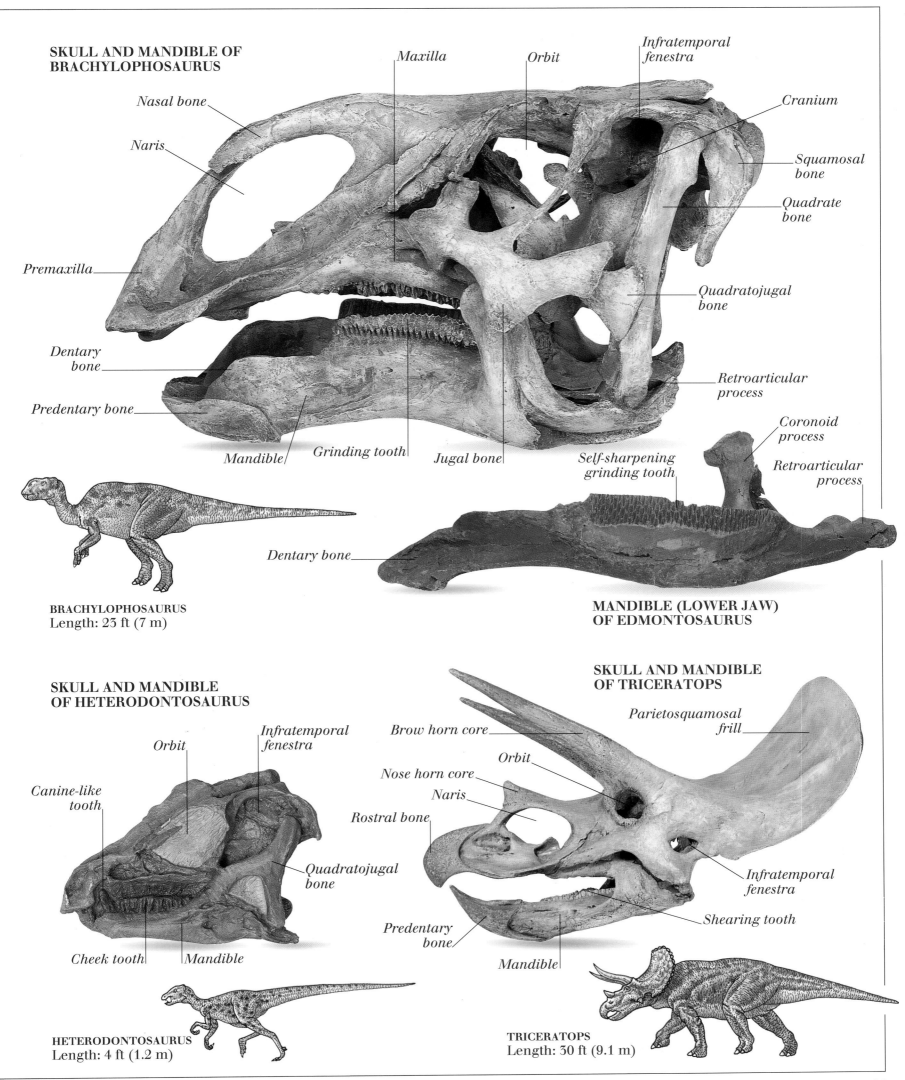

**SKULL AND MANDIBLE OF
BRACHYLOPHOSAURUS**

Nasal bone

Naris

Premaxilla

*Dentary
bone*

Predentary bone

Mandible

Grinding tooth

Maxilla

Orbit

*Infratemporal
fenestra*

Cranium

*Squamosal
bone*

*Quadrate
bone*

*Quadratojugal
bone*

*Retroarticular
process*

Jugal bone

*Self-sharpening
grinding tooth*

*Coronoid
process*

*Retroarticular
process*

Dentary bone

**MANDIBLE (LOWER JAW)
OF EDMONTOSAURUS**

BRACHYLOPHOSAURUS
Length: 23 ft (7 m)

**SKULL AND MANDIBLE
OF HETERODONTOSAURUS**

Orbit

*Infratemporal
fenestra*

*Canine-like
tooth*

*Quadratojugal
bone*

Cheek tooth

Mandible

HETERODONTOSAURUS
Length: 4 ft (1.2 m)

**SKULL AND MANDIBLE
OF TRICERATOPS**

Brow horn core

*Parietosquamosal
frill*

Nose horn core

Orbit

Naris

Rostral bone

*Infratemporal
fenestra*

*Predentary
bone*

Shearing tooth

Mandible

TRICERATOPS
Length: 30 ft (9.1 m)

Carnivores' heads

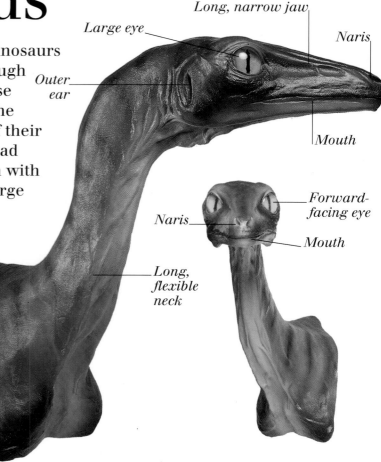

MOST CARNIVOROUS (FLESH-EATING) dinosaurs were probably active predators, although a few may have been scavengers; these flesh-eating life-styles are reflected in the features of their heads and the structure of their skulls. Carnivorous dinosaurs typically had strong jaws containing many sharp teeth with serrated edges to kill prey and tear off large chunks of flesh. As in many present-day carnivorous reptiles, the teeth of dinosaurs were replaced continually throughout their lifetime. Carnivorous dinosaurs did not have grinding teeth, which suggests that they swallowed food without chewing it. Some of their skulls had flexible joints, allowing them to distort slightly to accommodate huge mouthfuls of flesh. Typically, there were also many cavities in the skull, not only to minimize weight, but also to provide space for large, powerful jaw muscles. The heads and skulls of some carnivorous dinosaurs were adapted to specific diets. For example, *Baryonyx* had a crocodile-like skull that may have been adapted for catching fish, while *Oviraptor* had a deep, strong beak that might have been adapted for breaking into the shells of eggs or mollusks.

SKULL AND MANDIBLE OF DILOPHOSAURUS

HEAD OF TROODON

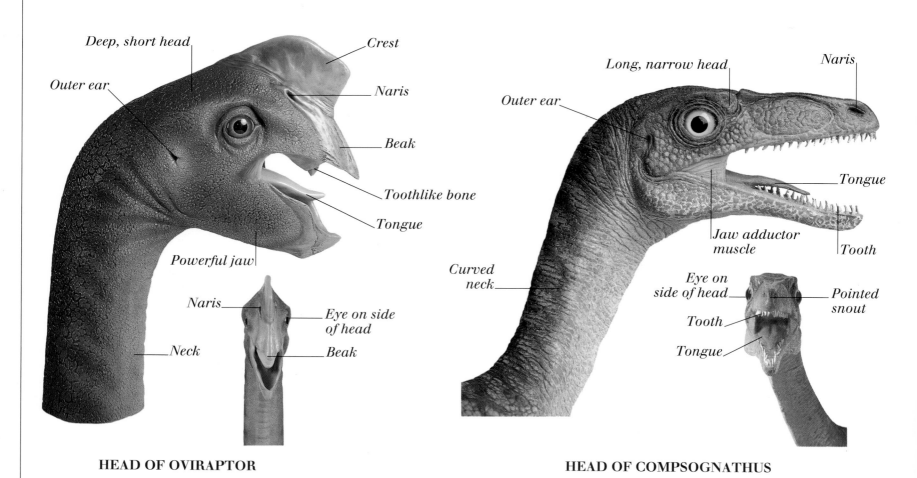

HEAD OF OVIRAPTOR

HEAD OF COMPSOGNATHUS

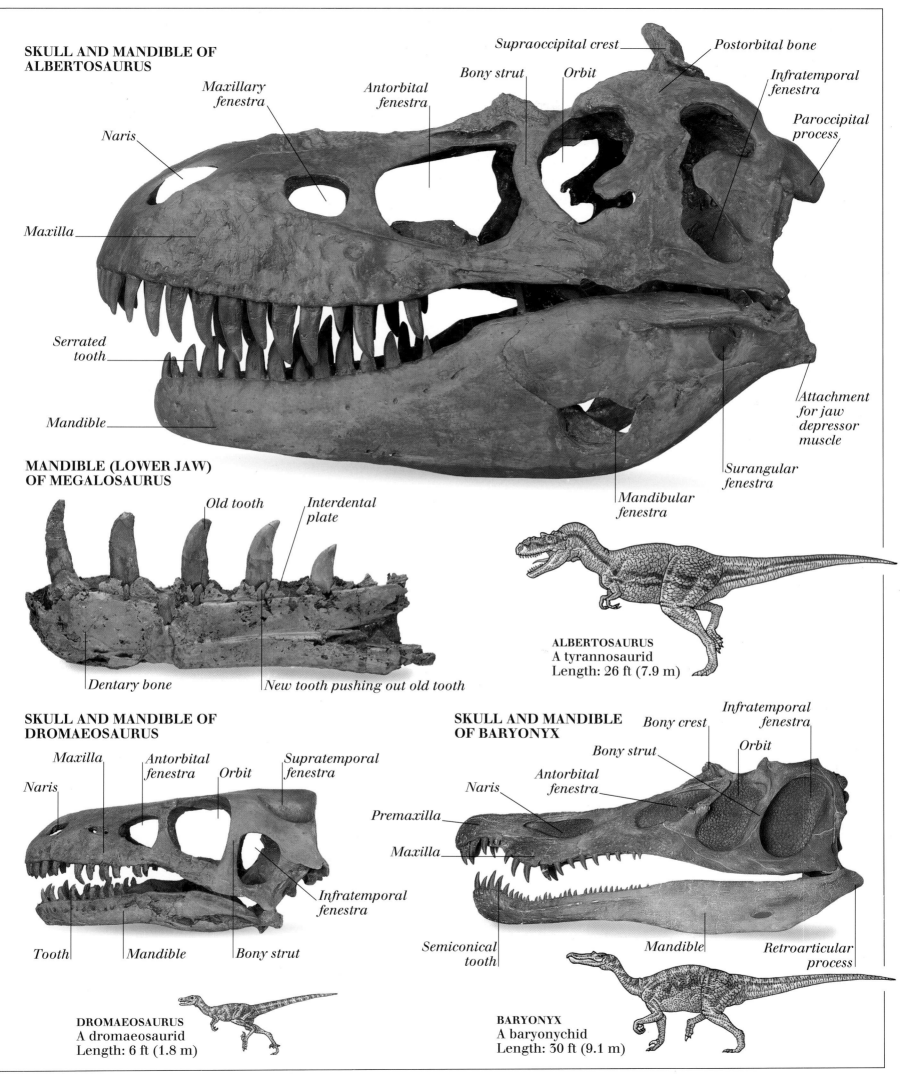

SKULL AND MANDIBLE OF ALBERTOSAURUS

Maxillary fenestra

Naris

Antorbital fenestra

Supraoccipital crest

Bony strut

Orbit

Postorbital bone

Infratemporal fenestra

Paroccipital process

Maxilla

Serrated tooth

Mandible

Attachment for jaw depressor muscle

Surangular fenestra

Mandibular fenestra

MANDIBLE (LOWER JAW) OF MEGALOSAURUS

Old tooth

Interdental plate

Dentary bone

New tooth pushing out old tooth

ALBERTOSAURUS
A tyrannosaurid
Length: 26 ft (7.9 m)

SKULL AND MANDIBLE OF DROMAEOSAURUS

Maxilla

Naris

Antorbital fenestra

Orbit

Supratemporal fenestra

Infratemporal fenestra

Tooth

Mandible

Bony strut

DROMAEOSAURUS
A dromaeosaurid
Length: 6 ft (1.8 m)

SKULL AND MANDIBLE OF BARYONYX

Bony crest

Infratemporal fenestra

Orbit

Bony strut

Antorbital fenestra

Naris

Premaxilla

Maxilla

Semiconical tooth

Mandible

Retroarticular process

BARYONYX
A baryonychid
Length: 30 ft (9.1 m)

33

Small ornithopods

SMALL ORNITHOPODS IS A GENERAL TERM for a varied collection
of ornithischian (bird-hipped), herbivorous (plant-eating)
dinosaurs that were widespread from Late Triassic to
Late Cretaceous times (231–65 million years ago). Most of these dinosaurs
were relatively small – typically less than about 13 ft (4 m) long. However, a
few were considerably larger. For example, *Tenontosaurus* was about 21 ft
(6.4 m) long. Large ornithopods, as their name suggests, were generally
bigger than small ornithopods and included iguanodonts (see pp. 36-37)
and hadrosaurs (see pp. 38-41). Most small ornithopods had the typical
ornithischian arrangement of a toothless beak and cheek teeth for grinding up
vegetation. However, the heterodontosaurids (meaning "different-tooth lizards")
had three distinct types of teeth – sharp cutting teeth at the front, two pairs of long,
canine-like teeth, and broad-ridged cheek teeth at the back of the mouth – an
arrangement that is extremely unusual for herbivores of any kind.

(see pp. 36-37)
(see pp. 38-41)

**EXAMPLES OF SMALL
ORNITHOPODS**

ORODROMEUS
A hypsilophodontid
Length: 8 ft (2.4 m)

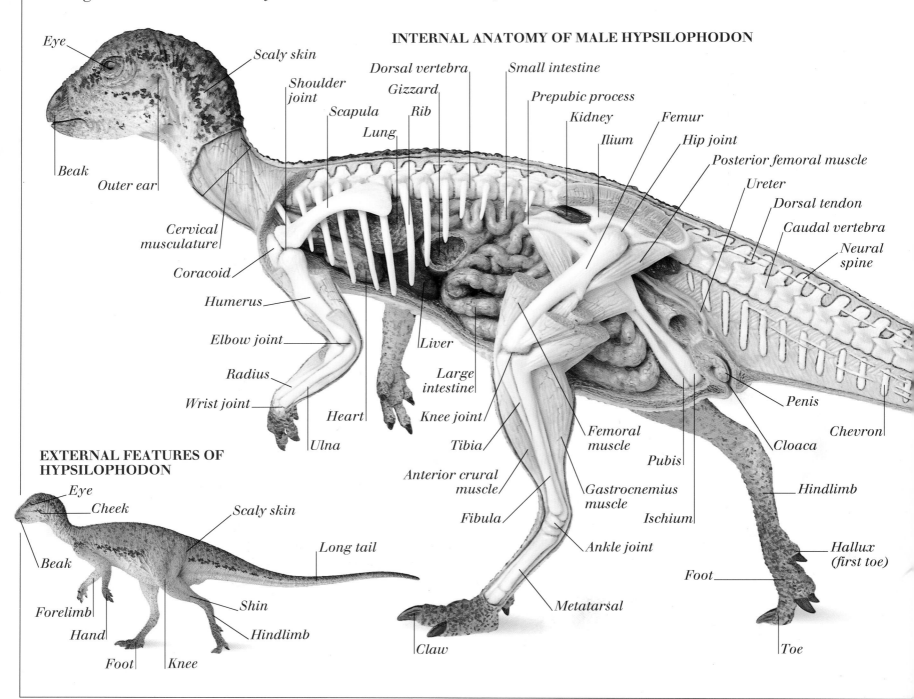

INTERNAL ANATOMY OF MALE HYPSILOPHODON

Eye

Scaly skin

Shoulder joint

Dorsal vertebra

Gizzard

Scapula

Rib

Lung

Small intestine

Prepubic process

Kidney

Femur

Ilium

Hip joint

Posterior femoral muscle

Ureter

Dorsal tendon

Caudal vertebra

Neural spine

Beak

Outer ear

Cervical musculature

Coracoid

Humerus

Elbow joint

Radius

Wrist joint

Heart

Liver

Large intestine

Knee joint

Ulna

Tibia

Anterior crural muscle

Fibula

Femoral muscle

Gastrocnemius muscle

Ischium

Ankle joint

Pubis

Metatarsal

Claw

Penis

Cloaca

Chevron

Hindlimb

Hallux (first toe)

Foot

Toe

**EXTERNAL FEATURES OF
HYPSILOPHODON**

Eye

Cheek

Scaly skin

Beak

Forelimb

Hand

Foot

Knee

Shin

Hindlimb

Long tail

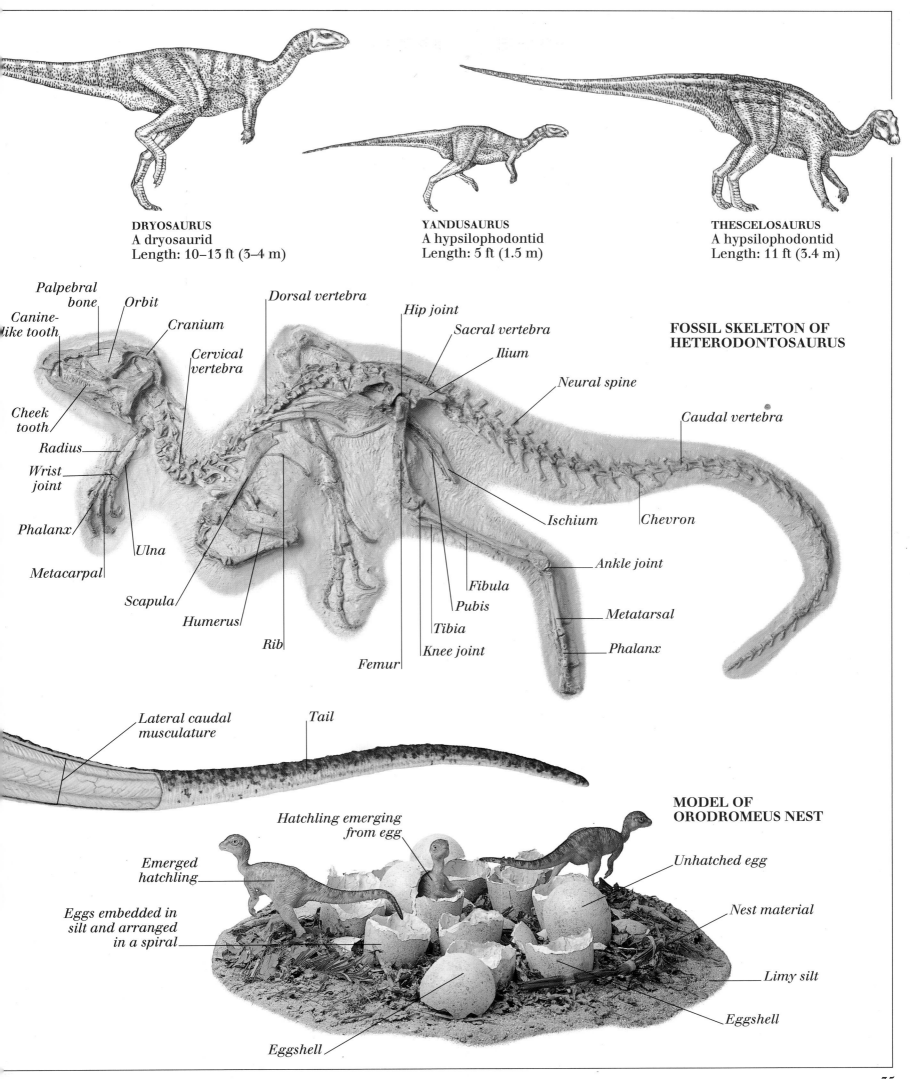

DRYOSAURUS
A dryosaurid
Length: 10–13 ft (3–4 m)

YANDUSAURUS
A hypsilophodontid
Length: 5 ft (1.5 m)

THESCELOSAURUS
A hypsilophodontid
Length: 11 ft (3.4 m)

**FOSSIL SKELETON OF
HETERODONTOSAURUS**

Palpebral
bone

Orbit

Canine-
like tooth

Cranium

Dorsal vertebra

Hip joint

Sacral vertebra

Ilium

Cervical
vertebra

Neural spine

Caudal vertebra

Cheek
tooth

Radius

Wrist
joint

Phalanx

Ischium

Chevron

Metacarpal

Ulna

Scapula

Humerus

Rib

Femur

Knee joint

Tibia

Pubis

Fibula

Ankle joint

Metatarsal

Phalanx

Lateral caudal
musculature

Tail

**MODEL OF
ORODROMEUS NEST**

Hatchling emerging
from egg

Emerged
hatchling

Unhatched egg

Eggs embedded in
silt and arranged
in a spiral

Nest material

Limy silt

Eggshell

Eggshell

Iguanodonts

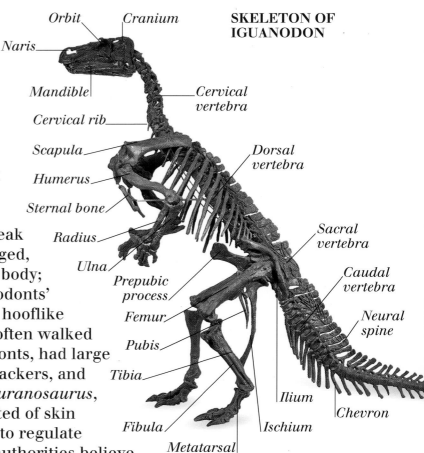

IGUANODONTS WERE A GROUP of herbivorous (plant-eating), ornithischian (bird-hipped) dinosaurs that lived from Late Jurassic to Late Cretaceous times (165–70 million years ago). They were medium- to large-size dinosaurs – between 11 ft 6 in (3.5 m) and 33 ft (10 m) long – and lived in what are now North America, Europe, Africa, Asia, and Australia. Typically, iguanodonts had a broad, toothless beak at the end of a long snout; large jaws with long rows of ridged, close-packed cheek teeth, for grinding vegetation; a bulky body; and a heavy tail that was stiffened by bony tendons. Iguanodonts' powerful hindlimbs enabled them to run from danger, but hooflike nails on their fingers and toes indicate that they probably often walked on all fours. *Iguanodon*, and probably some other iguanodonts, had large thumb spikes that were probably strong enough to stab attackers, and flexible little fingers. The most unusual iguanodont was *Ouranosaurus*, which had a "sail" along its back. The sail probably consisted of skin stretched tightly over upright spines and may have served to regulate body temperature by absorbing and radiating heat. Some authorities believe that all iguanodonts belong to one group, the iguanodontids. However, others divide them into two subgroups: iguanodontids, such as *Iguanodon*, *Ouranosaurus*, and *Probactrosaurus*, and camptosaurids, such as *Camptosaurus* and possibly *Muttaburrasaurus*. This division is based on the number of toes of the dinosaurs: iguanodontids had three toes, while camptosaurids had four.

IGUANODON TOOTH

Orbit · Cranium · Naris · Mandible · Cervical vertebra · Cervical rib · Scapula · Humerus · Sternal bone · Radius · Ulna · Dorsal vertebra · Prepubic process · Femur · Pubis · Sacral vertebra · Caudal vertebra · Neural spine · Tibia · Ilium · Chevron · Fibula · Ischium · Metatarsal

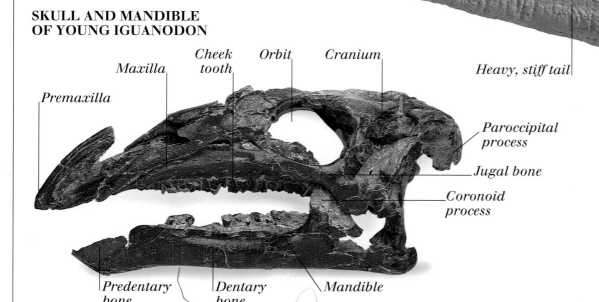

Thigh · Heavy, stiff tail · Knee · Hindlimb · Ankle · Toe · Foot · Hooflike nail

**SKULL AND MANDIBLE
OF YOUNG IGUANODON**

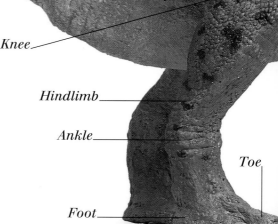

Maxilla · Cheek tooth · Orbit · Cranium · Premaxilla · Paroccipital process · Jugal bone · Coronoid process · Predentary bone · Dentary bone · Mandible

EXAMPLES OF IGUANODONTS

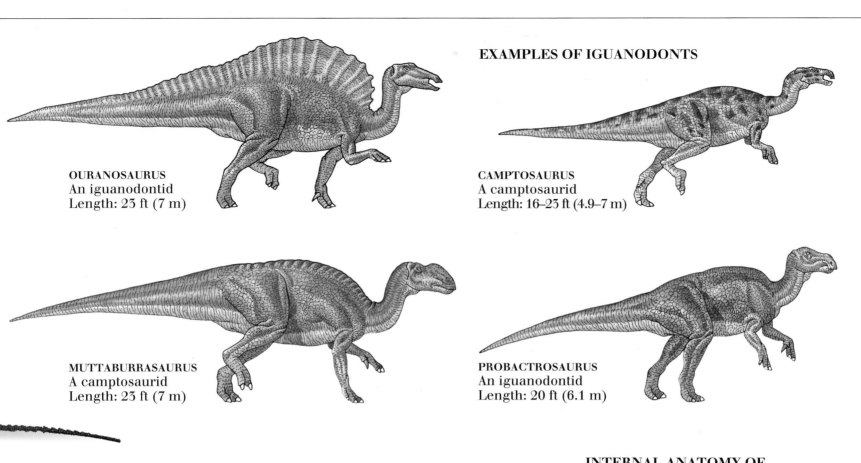

OURANOSAURUS
An iguanodontid
Length: 23 ft (7 m)

CAMPTOSAURUS
A camptosaurid
Length: 16–23 ft (4.9–7 m)

MUTTABURRASAURUS
A camptosaurid
Length: 23 ft (7 m)

PROBACTROSAURUS
An iguanodontid
Length: 20 ft (6.1 m)

EXTERNAL FEATURES OF IGUANODON

INTERNAL ANATOMY OF HIND LEG OF IGUANODON

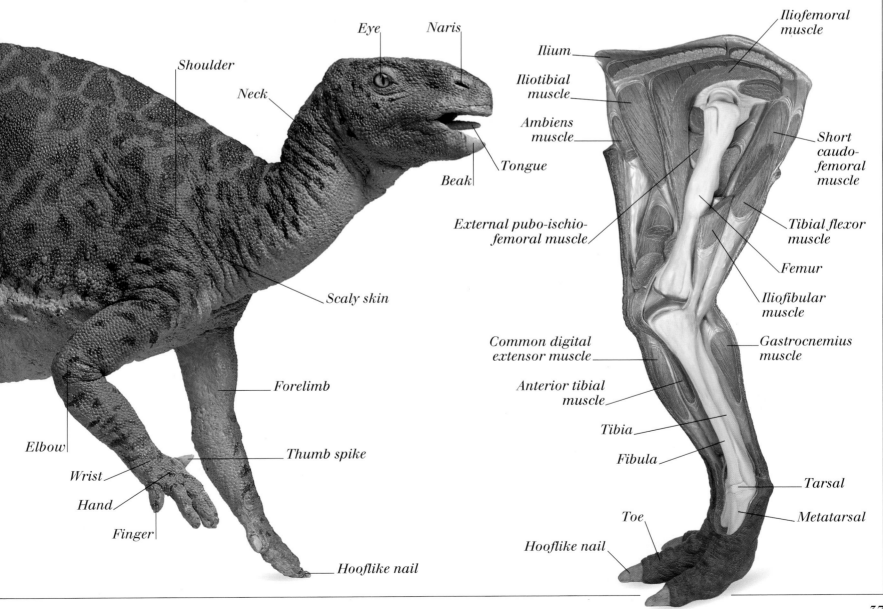

Eye

Naris

Shoulder

Neck

Tongue

Beak

Scaly skin

Forelimb

Elbow

Wrist

Hand

Finger

Thumb spike

Hooflike nail

Ilium

Iliofemoral muscle

Iliotibial muscle

Ambiens muscle

Short caudo-femoral muscle

External pubo-ischio-femoral muscle

Tibial flexor muscle

Femur

Iliofibular muscle

Gastrocnemius muscle

Common digital extensor muscle

Anterior tibial muscle

Tibia

Fibula

Tarsal

Metatarsal

Toe

Hooflike nail

Hadrosaurs 1

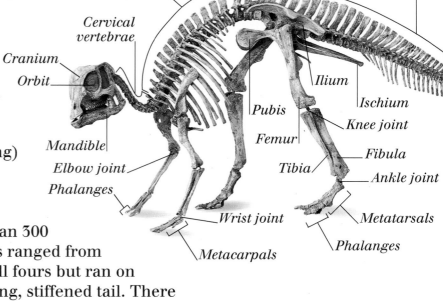

Sacral vertebrae

Caudal vertebrae

Dorsal vertebrae

Cervical vertebrae

Cranium

Orbit

Ilium

Ischium

Pubis

Knee joint

Femur

Mandible

Fibula

Elbow joint

Tibia

Ankle joint

Phalanges

Wrist joint

Metatarsals

Metacarpals

Phalanges

FOSSIL SKELETON OF YOUNG HADROSAUR

HADROSAURS WERE a group of ornithischian (bird-hipped) dinosaurs that lived during Late Cretaceous times (97.5–65 million years ago) in what are now North America, Asia, and Europe. A characteristic feature of these herbivorous (plant-eating) dinosaurs was a beak similar to a duck's bill, which is the reason why hadrosaurs are sometimes known as duckbills. Although the beak was toothless, hadrosaurs had large numbers of cheek teeth – sometimes more than 300 in each jaw – for grinding tough vegetation. Hadrosaurs ranged from 13 ft (4 m) to 49 ft (14.9 m) in length. They walked on all fours but ran on their hind limbs, balancing their heavy bodies with a long, stiffened tail. There were two main subgroups of hadrosaurs: hadrosaurines, such as *Gryposaurus* and *Maiasaura*, and lambeosaurines, such as *Corythosaurus* and *Parasaurolophus*. The main difference between the subgroups was the shape of the skull. Hadrosaurines had flat skulls, some with bumps of solid bone on the snout, while the skulls of lambeosaurines had large, hollow, bony crests.

FOSSIL SKELETON OF GRYPOSAURUS

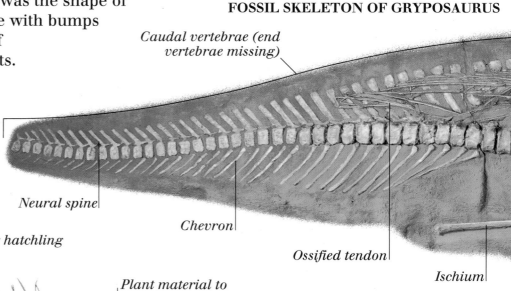

Caudal vertebrae (end vertebrae missing)

Neural spine

Chevron

Ossified tendon

Ischium

MODEL OF MAIASAURA NEST

Rounded top end of egg

Emerging hatchling

Hatchling

Eggshell fragment

Plant material to protect and warm eggs

Raised nest made of sand

Unhatched egg

Ankle joint

EXAMPLES OF HADROSAURINES

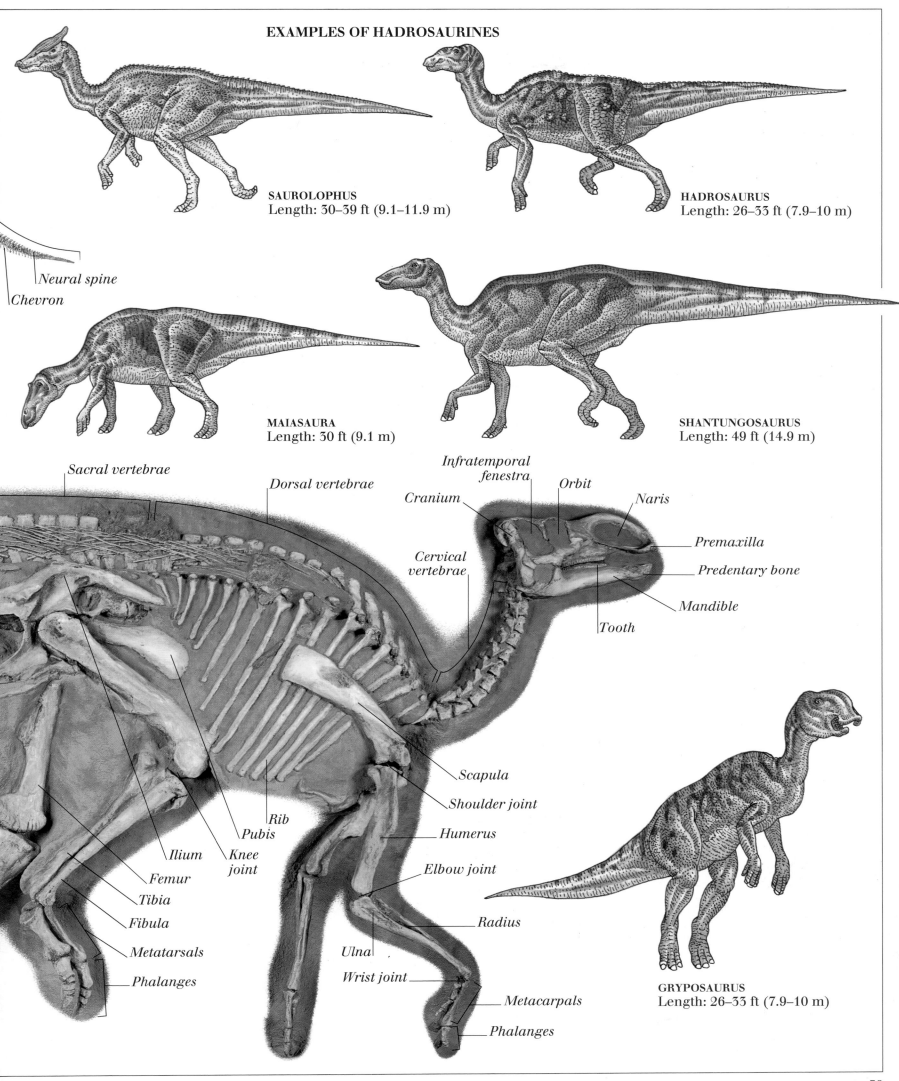

SAUROLOPHUS
Length: 30–39 ft (9.1–11.9 m)

HADROSAURUS
Length: 26–33 ft (7.9–10 m)

Neural spine

Chevron

MAIASAURA
Length: 30 ft (9.1 m)

SHANTUNGOSAURUS
Length: 49 ft (14.9 m)

Sacral vertebrae

Dorsal vertebrae

Infratemporal fenestra

Cranium

Orbit

Naris

Cervical vertebrae

Premaxilla

Predentary bone

Mandible

Tooth

Scapula

Shoulder joint

Humerus

Elbow joint

Radius

Ulna

Wrist joint

Metacarpals

Phalanges

Rib

Pubis

Ilium

Knee joint

Femur

Tibia

Fibula

Metatarsals

Phalanges

GRYPOSAURUS
Length: 26–33 ft (7.9–10 m)

39

Hadrosaurs 2

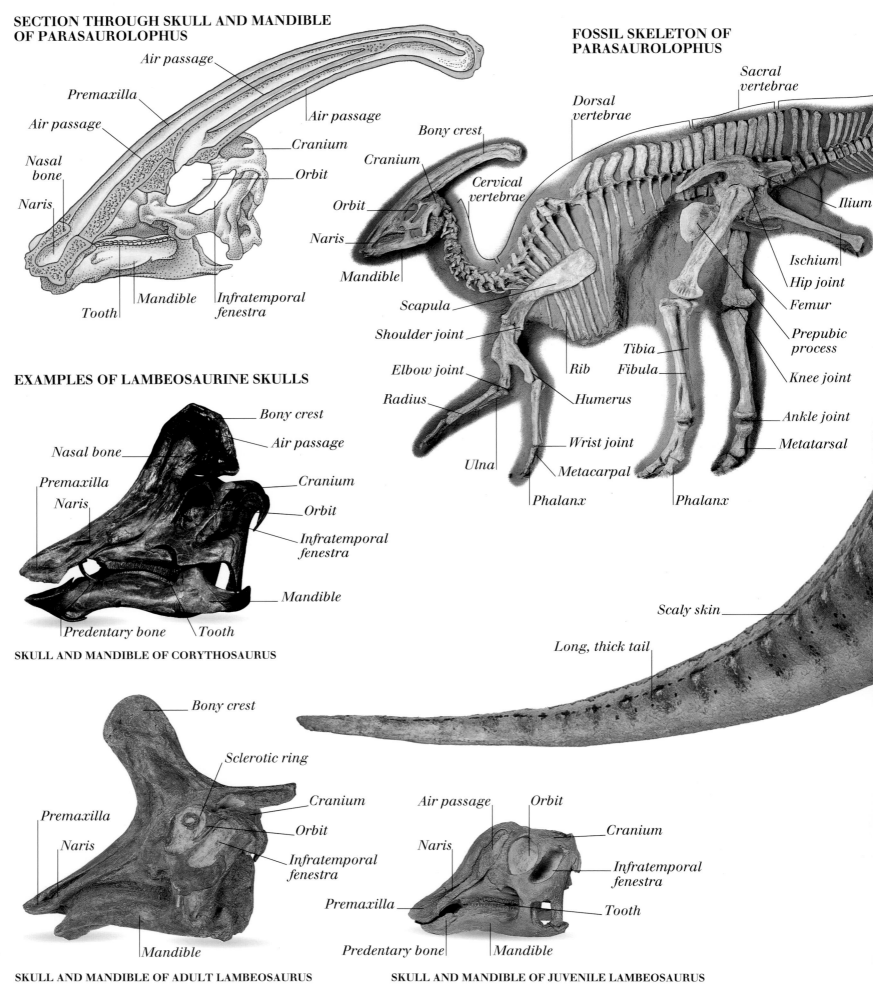

SECTION THROUGH SKULL AND MANDIBLE OF PARASAUROLOPHUS

Air passage
Premaxilla
Air passage
Air passage
Nasal bone
Cranium
Naris
Orbit
Tooth
Mandible
Infratemporal fenestra

FOSSIL SKELETON OF PARASAUROLOPHUS

Sacral vertebrae
Dorsal vertebrae
Bony crest
Cranium
Cervical vertebrae
Orbit
Naris
Ilium
Mandible
Ischium
Scapula
Hip joint
Shoulder joint
Femur
Elbow joint
Prepubic process
Radius
Rib
Tibia
Fibula
Knee joint
Humerus
Ankle joint
Wrist joint
Metatarsal
Ulna
Metacarpal
Phalanx
Phalanx

EXAMPLES OF LAMBEOSAURINE SKULLS

Bony crest
Nasal bone
Air passage
Premaxilla
Cranium
Naris
Orbit
Infratemporal fenestra
Mandible
Predentary bone
Tooth

SKULL AND MANDIBLE OF CORYTHOSAURUS

Scaly skin
Long, thick tail

Bony crest
Sclerotic ring
Premaxilla
Cranium
Naris
Orbit
Infratemporal fenestra
Mandible

Air passage
Orbit
Cranium
Naris
Infratemporal fenestra
Premaxilla
Tooth
Predentary bone
Mandible

SKULL AND MANDIBLE OF ADULT LAMBEOSAURUS

SKULL AND MANDIBLE OF JUVENILE LAMBEOSAURUS

EXTERNAL FEATURES OF CORYTHOSAURUS

Bony crest

Eye

Naris

Toothless beak

Caudal vertebrae

Cheek pouch

Tongue

Neural spine

Neck

Chevron

Shoulder

Forelimb

Elbow

Wrist

Hand

Finger

Knee

Nail

Thigh

Tubercle

Hindlimb

Ankle

Foot

Toe

Nail

EXAMPLES OF LAMBEOSAURINES

CORYTHOSAURUS
Length: 33 ft (10 m)

PARASAUROLOPHUS
Length: 33 ft (10 m)

HYPACROSAURUS
Length: 30 ft (9.1 m)

LAMBEOSAURUS
Length: 49 ft (14.9 m)

Stegosaurs

STEGOSAURS WERE A GROUP of ornithischian (bird-hipped) dinosaurs that lived from Middle Jurassic to Early Cretaceous times (188–97.5 million years ago) in what are now North America, Europe, Africa, and Asia. They were medium-size dinosaurs – between about 10 ft (3 m) and 30 ft (9.1 m) long – with bulky bodies that weighed up to about 1.5 tons. The main characteristic of stegosaurs was the two rows of dorsal plates or spines that ran along their backs. The exact function of these plates or spikes is not known, but it is thought that they may have been for defense, for display, or for regulating body temperature by absorbing or radiating heat. Also, probably for defense, stegosaurs had caudal (tail) spikes and, in some species, shoulder spikes. There were two main subgroups of stegosaurs: stegosaurids, such as *Stegosaurus*, *Tuojiangosaurus*, *Kentrosaurus*, and *Wuerhosaurus*, and huayangosaurids. *Huayangosaurus*, the only known huayangosaurid, resembled stegosaurids but is thought to have been more primitive.

EXAMPLES OF STEGOSAURS

WUERHOSAURUS
A stegosaurid
Length: 20 ft (6.1 m)

TOP VIEW OF STEGOSAURUS

EXTERNAL FEATURES OF STEGOSAURUS

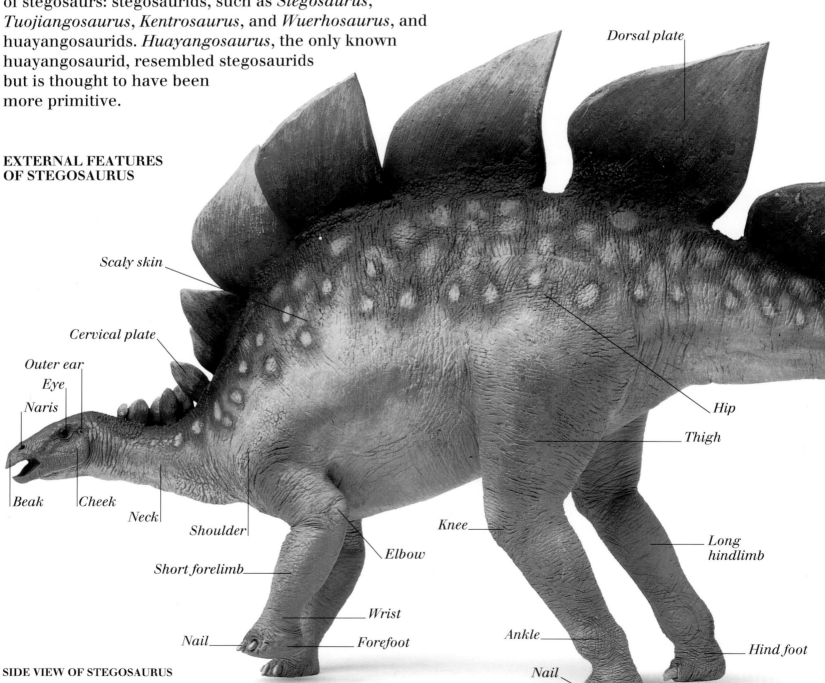

SIDE VIEW OF STEGOSAURUS

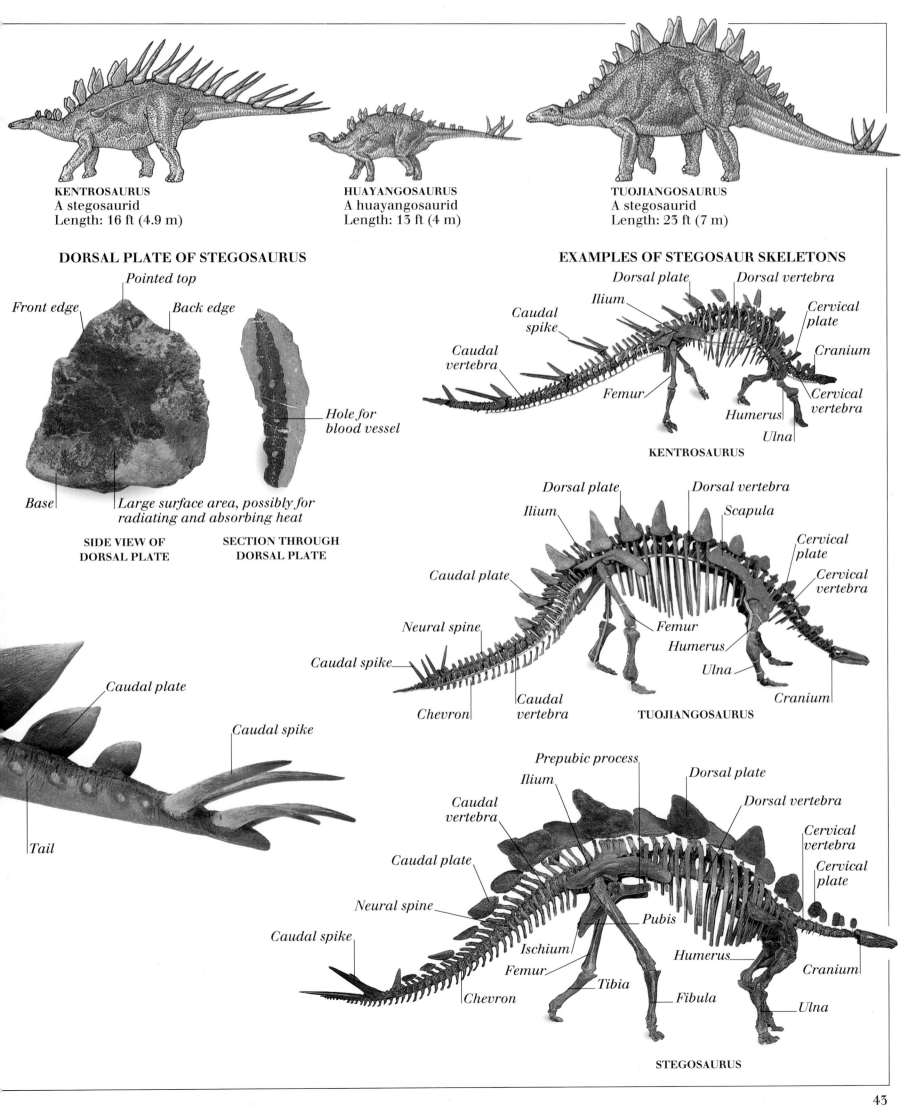

KENTROSAURUS
A stegosaurid
Length: 16 ft (4.9 m)

HUAYANGOSAURUS
A huayangosaurid
Length: 13 ft (4 m)

TUOJIANGOSAURUS
A stegosaurid
Length: 23 ft (7 m)

DORSAL PLATE OF STEGOSAURUS

Pointed top

Front edge

Back edge

Hole for blood vessel

Base

Large surface area, possibly for radiating and absorbing heat

SIDE VIEW OF DORSAL PLATE

SECTION THROUGH DORSAL PLATE

EXAMPLES OF STEGOSAUR SKELETONS

Dorsal plate

Dorsal vertebra

Ilium

Cervical plate

Caudal spike

Cranium

Caudal vertebra

Cervical vertebra

Femur

Humerus

Ulna

KENTROSAURUS

Dorsal plate

Dorsal vertebra

Ilium

Scapula

Cervical plate

Caudal plate

Cervical vertebra

Neural spine

Femur

Caudal spike

Humerus

Ulna

Chevron

Caudal vertebra

Cranium

TUOJIANGOSAURUS

Caudal plate

Caudal spike

Tail

Prepubic process

Ilium

Dorsal plate

Caudal vertebra

Dorsal vertebra

Caudal plate

Cervical vertebra

Cervical plate

Neural spine

Pubis

Caudal spike

Ischium

Humerus

Femur

Cranium

Tibia

Fibula

Ulna

Chevron

STEGOSAURUS

43

Ankylosaurs

ANKYLOSAURS WERE A GROUP OF HERBIVOROUS (plant-eating), ornithischian (bird-hipped) dinosaurs that lived from Middle Jurassic to Late Cretaceous times (188–65 million years ago) in what are now Mongolia, North America, Antarctica, Australia, and Europe. They ranged from 8 ft (2.4 m) to 35 ft (10.7 m) long, and weighed up to 2 tons.

The most notable feature of these dinosaurs was their heavy armor, which consisted of bony studs, plates, and spikes that protected them from predators. Ankylosaurs also had characteristics typical of herbivorous dinosaurs: toothless beaks and cheek teeth, for cropping and chewing vegetation. It is possible that ankylosaurs also had a gizzard (muscular stomach) and gastroliths (stones) for further breaking down plant material in the gut. There were two main subgroups of ankylosaurs: ankylosaurids, such as *Ankylosaurus*, *Euoplocephalus*, and *Pinacosaurus*; and nodosaurids, such as *Edmontonia*, *Minmi*, *Panoplosaurus*, and *Polacanthus*. The most apparent differences between the subgroups were that ankylosaurids had horns on their head and a bony tail club, while nodosaurids tended to have neither.

SHOULDER SPIKE OF POLACANTHUS

EXAMPLES OF ANKYLOSAURS

MINMI
A nodosaurid
Length: 8 ft (2.4 m)

FOSSIL OF ANKYLOSAURUS TAIL CLUB

Ossified caudal vertebra

Lateral plate

Terminal plate

INTERNAL ANATOMY OF FEMALE EUOPLOCEPHALUS

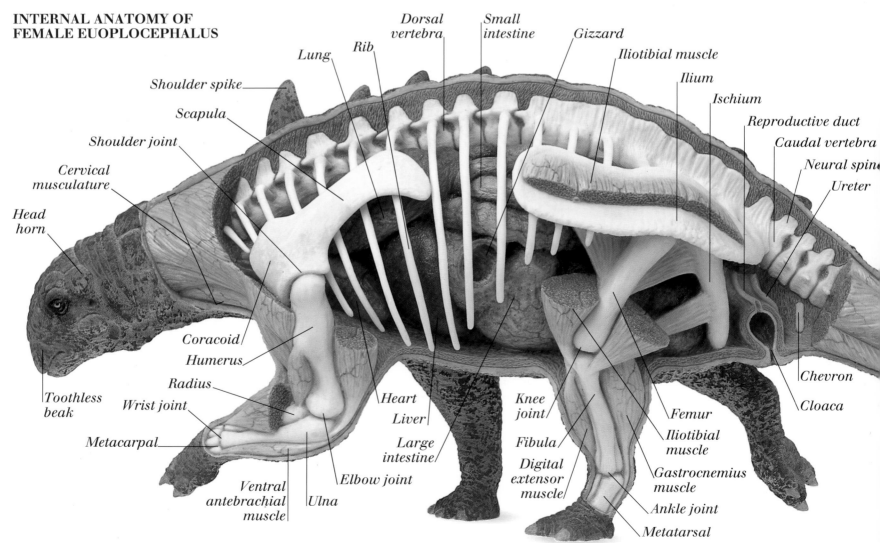

Dorsal vertebra

Small intestine

Gizzard

Iliotibial muscle

Ilium

Ischium

Reproductive duct

Caudal vertebra

Neural spine

Ureter

Lung

Rib

Shoulder spike

Scapula

Shoulder joint

Cervical musculature

Head horn

Coracoid

Humerus

Radius

Wrist joint

Toothless beak

Metacarpal

Ventral antebrachial muscle

Ulna

Elbow joint

Heart

Liver

Large intestine

Knee joint

Fibula

Digital extensor muscle

Femur

Iliotibial muscle

Gastrocnemius muscle

Ankle joint

Metatarsal

Chevron

Cloaca

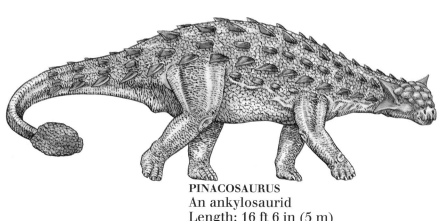

PINACOSAURUS
An ankylosaurid
Length: 16 ft 6 in (5 m)

POLACANTHUS
A nodosaurid
Length: 13 ft (4 m)

EXTERNAL FEATURES OF EDMONTONIA

EXAMPLES OF ANKYLOSAUR SKULLS

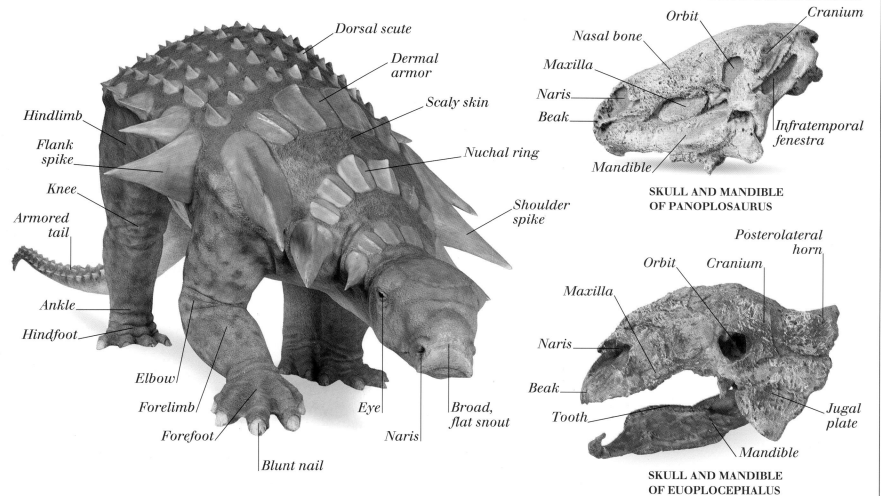

Dorsal scute

Dermal armor

Scaly skin

Nuchal ring

Shoulder spike

Hindlimb

Flank spike

Knee

Armored tail

Ankle

Hindfoot

Elbow

Forelimb

Forefoot

Blunt nail

Eye

Naris

Broad, flat snout

Orbit

Cranium

Nasal bone

Maxilla

Naris

Beak

Infratemporal fenestra

Mandible

SKULL AND MANDIBLE OF PANOPLOSAURUS

Posterolateral horn

Orbit

Cranium

Maxilla

Naris

Beak

Tooth

Jugal plate

Mandible

SKULL AND MANDIBLE OF EUOPLOCEPHALUS

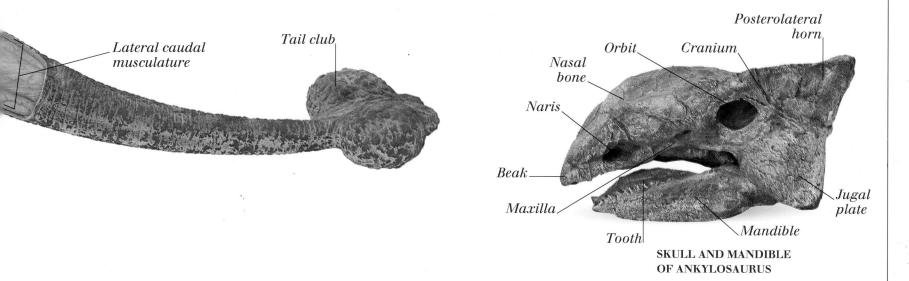

Lateral caudal musculature

Tail club

Posterolateral horn

Orbit

Cranium

Nasal bone

Naris

Beak

Maxilla

Tooth

Mandible

Jugal plate

SKULL AND MANDIBLE OF ANKYLOSAURUS

45

Pachycephalosaurs

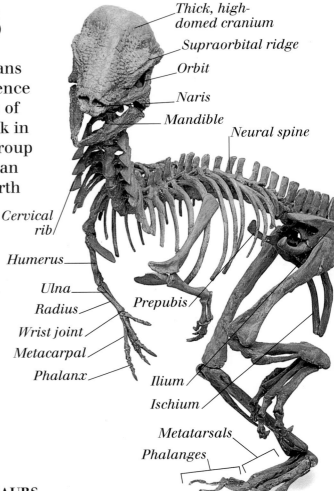

THE TERM "pachycephalosaur" means "thick-headed lizard," a reference to the extremely thick-roofed skulls of these dinosaurs – up to 10 in (25 cm) thick in some cases. Pachycephalosaurs were a group of herbivorous (plant-eating), ornithischian (bird-hipped) dinosaurs that lived predominantly in what are now North America, Madagascar, China, and Mongolia in Late Cretaceous times (97.5–65 million years ago). Their thick skulls were probably designed to protect their brains during head-butting contests to win territory and mates; their hips and spine were also strengthened to withstand the shock of head-butting. Pachycephalosaurs ranged from about 20 in (50 cm) to 15 ft (4.6 m) in length. They had short arms, long, stiff tails to aid balance, and thickset bodies. There were two main subgroups of pachycephalosaurs: pachycephalosaurids, such as *Pachycephalosaurus*, *Stegoceras*, and *Prenocephale*, and homalocephalids, such as *Homalocephale* and *Wannanosaurus*. Pachycephalosaurids had thick, high-domed skulls that could withstand heavier blows than the less thick, flat-topped skulls of homalocephalids.

HEAD-BUTTING PRENOCEPHALES

Thick, high-domed cranium
Supraorbital ridge
Orbit
Naris
Mandible
Neural spine
Cervical rib
Humerus
Ulna
Radius
Prepubis
Wrist joint
Metacarpal
Phalanx
Ilium
Ischium
Metatarsals
Phalanges

EXAMPLES OF SKULLS OF PACHYCEPHALOSAURS

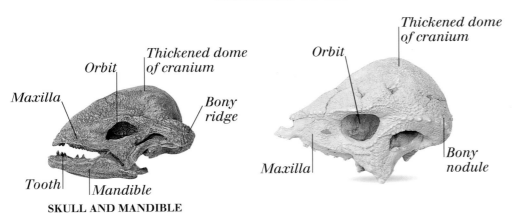

Orbit
Thickened dome of cranium
Maxilla
Bony ridge
Tooth
Mandible

SKULL AND MANDIBLE OF STEGOCERAS

Thickened dome of cranium
Orbit
Maxilla
Bony nodule

SKULL OF PRENOCEPHALE

Thickened dome of cranium
Bony spike
Maxilla
Orbit
Bony nodule

SKULL OF PACHYCEPHALOSAURUS

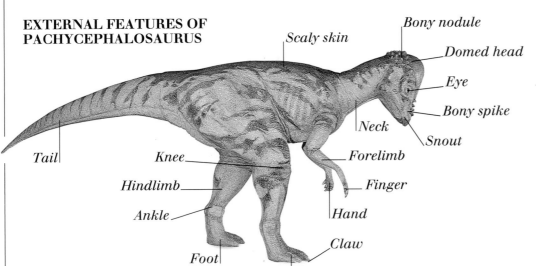

EXTERNAL FEATURES OF PACHYCEPHALOSAURUS

Scaly skin
Bony nodule
Domed head
Eye
Bony spike
Neck
Snout
Tail
Knee
Forelimb
Hindlimb
Finger
Ankle
Hand
Foot
Claw
Toe

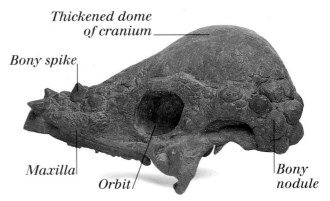

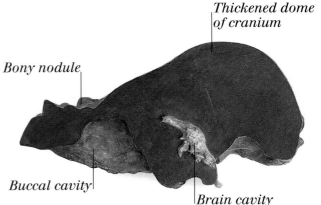

Thickened dome of cranium
Bony nodule
Buccal cavity
Brain cavity

SECTION THROUGH SKULL OF PACHYCEPHALOSAURUS

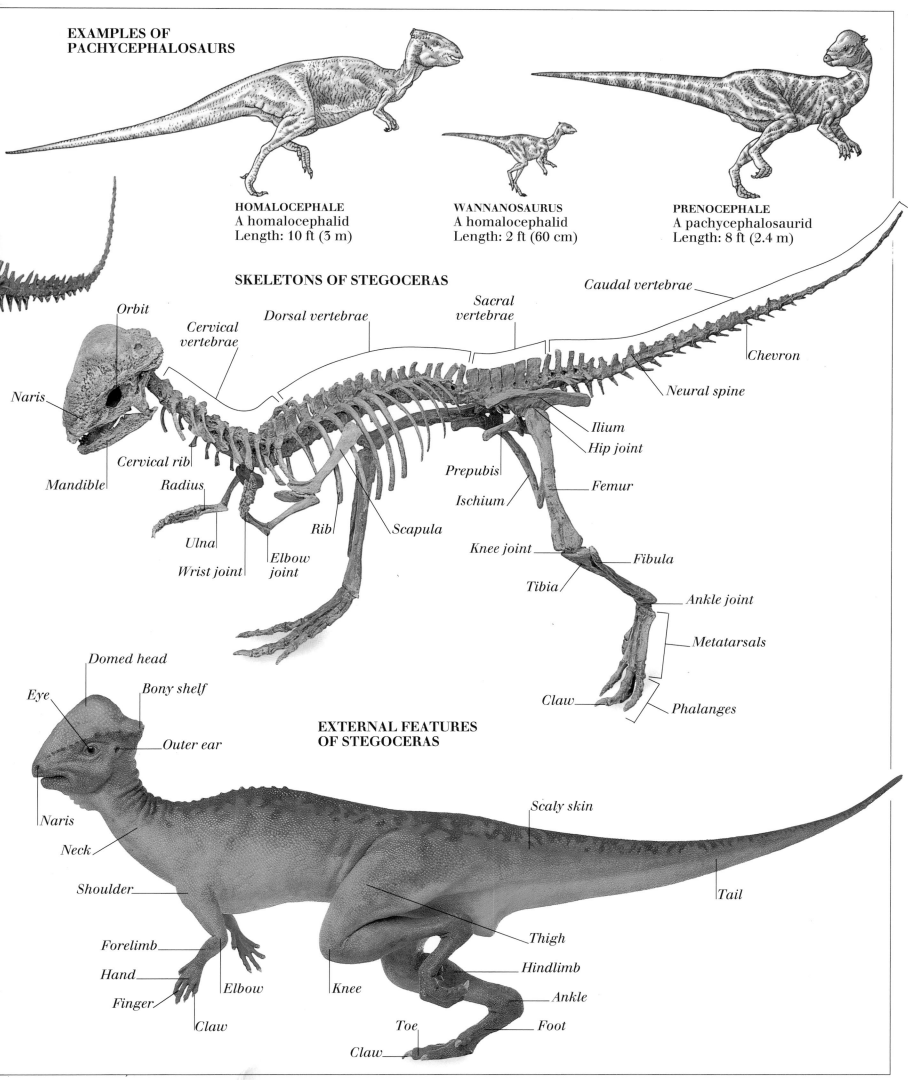

EXAMPLES OF PACHYCEPHALOSAURS

HOMALOCEPHALE
A homalocephalid
Length: 10 ft (3 m)

WANNANOSAURUS
A homalocephalid
Length: 2 ft (60 cm)

PRENOCEPHALE
A pachycephalosaurid
Length: 8 ft (2.4 m)

SKELETONS OF STEGOCERAS

Orbit

Cervical
vertebrae

Dorsal vertebrae

Sacral
vertebrae

Caudal vertebrae

Naris

Chevron

Neural spine

Ilium

Hip joint

Cervical rib

Prepubis

Femur

Mandible

Ischium

Radius

Rib

Scapula

Ulna

Knee joint

Fibula

Wrist joint

Elbow
joint

Tibia

Ankle joint

Metatarsals

Claw

Phalanges

**EXTERNAL FEATURES
OF STEGOCERAS**

Domed head

Bony shelf

Eye

Outer ear

Naris

Scaly skin

Neck

Shoulder

Tail

Forelimb

Thigh

Hand

Hindlimb

Finger

Elbow

Knee

Ankle

Claw

Foot

Toe

Claw

Ceratopsians 1

CERATOPSIANS WERE A GROUP of ornithischian (bird-hipped), herbivorous (plant-eating) dinosaurs with short, deep, parrot-like beaks. These dinosaurs flourished during the Cretaceous period (144–65 million years ago). There were three subgroups of ceratopsians: protoceratopsids, ceratopsids, and psittacosaurids. Protoceratopsids, such as *Protoceratops*, *Bagaceratops,* and *Microceratops*, were relatively small, ranging from 30 in (76 cm) to 10 ft (3 m) long. They had a bony frill around the neck that may have been used to frighten predators, protect the neck, or attract mates; the frill may also have served as an anchor for the jaw muscles. Some species of protoceratopsid also had brow ridges and small horns on their noses and cheeks. Ceratopsids, such as *Triceratops, Torosaurus, Styracosaurus, Pachyrhinosaurus*, and *Eucentrosaurus,* were larger than protoceratopsids, ranging from 6 ft (1.8 m) to 30 ft (9.1 m) in length. *Triceratops*, one of the largest ceratopsids, had a massive head and bulky body, and weighed up to about 5.4 tons. Ceratopsids had neck frills that were larger than those of protoceratopsids, and horns on their brow and nose. In some cases, ceratopsid brow horns were up to 3 ft (90 cm) long. *Psittacosaurus*, the only psittacosaurid known, was 6 ft 6 in (2 m) long. In addition to the parrot-like ceratopsian beak, it had small cheek horns; however, it did not have a bony neck frill.

NEST AND EGGS OF PROTOCERATOPS

SECTION THROUGH CERATOPSIAN EGG

Yolk sac
Embryo
Amniotic sac
Allantois
Chorion
Shell

SKULL AND MANDIBLE OF PROTOCERATOPS

Parietosquamosal frill
Cranium
Postorbital bone
Orbit
Nasal bone
Lacrimal bone
Naris
Beak
Rostral bone
Predentary bone
Dentary bone
Tooth
Parietal fenestra
Infratemporal fenestra
Jugal bone
Surangular bone
Angular bone
Mandible
Tail

FOSSIL SKELETON OF PROTOCERATOPS

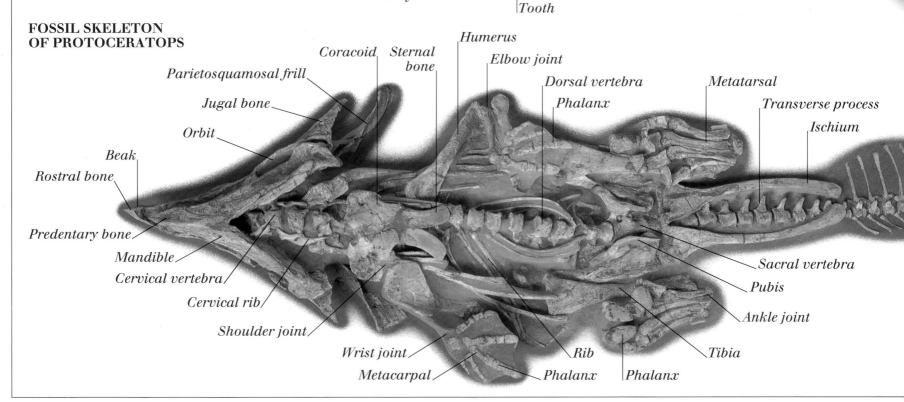

Coracoid
Sternal bone
Humerus
Elbow joint
Parietosquamosal frill
Jugal bone
Orbit
Beak
Rostral bone
Predentary bone
Mandible
Cervical vertebra
Cervical rib
Shoulder joint
Wrist joint
Metacarpal
Dorsal vertebra
Phalanx
Metatarsal
Transverse process
Ischium
Sacral vertebra
Pubis
Ankle joint
Tibia
Rib
Phalanx
Phalanx

EXTERNAL FEATURES OF PSITTACOSAURUS

Eye

Outer ear

Cheek horn

Beak

Claw

Finger

Forelimb

Claw

Elbow

Knee

Toe

Ankle

Hindlimb

Thigh

Neural spine

Chevron

Caudal vertebra

SKULL AND MANDIBLE OF PSITTACOSAURUS

Orbit

Infratemporal fenestra

Naris

Beak

Jugal bone

Rostral bone

Predentary bone

Mandible

EXAMPLES OF PROTOCERATOPSIDS

MICROCERATOPS
Length: 30 in (76 cm)

BAGACERATOPS
Length: 3 ft 3 in (1 m)

LEPTOCERATOPS
Length: 7 ft (2.1 m)

PROTOCERATOPS
Length: 9 ft (2.7 m)

Ceratopsians 2

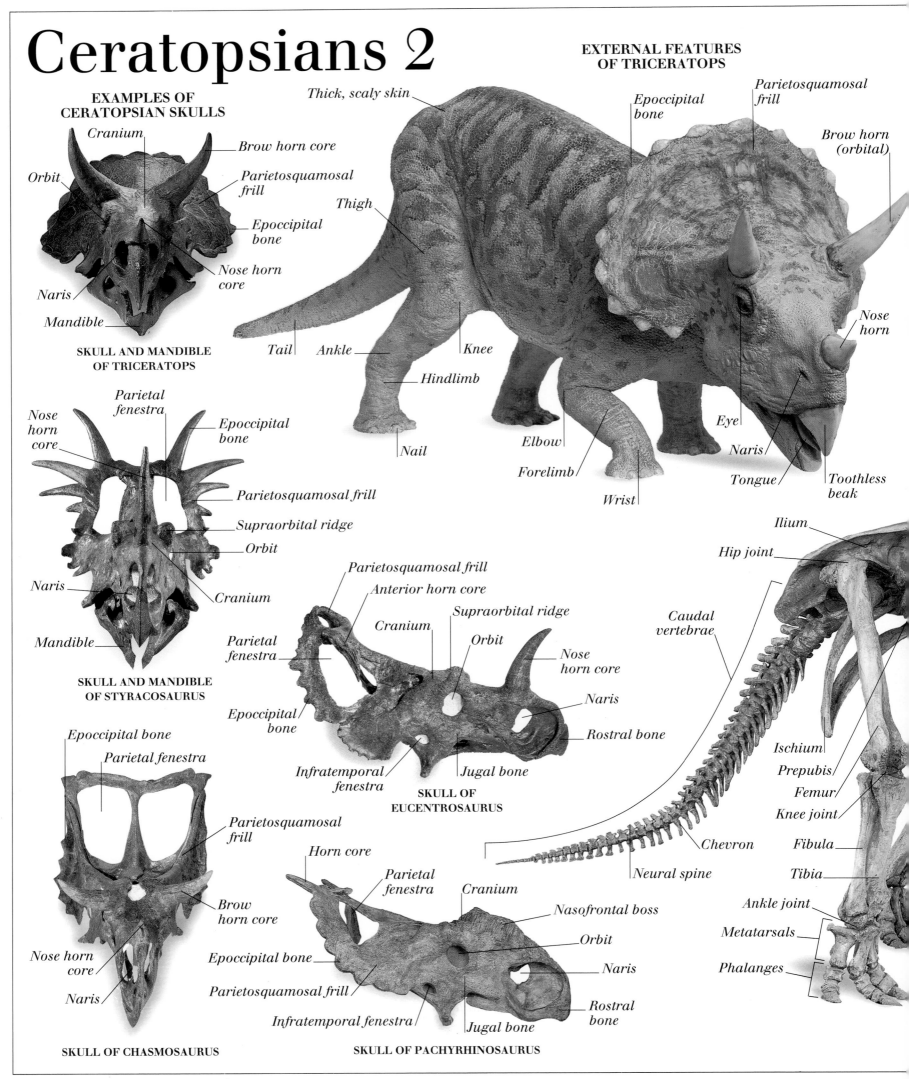

**EXAMPLES OF
CERATOPSIAN SKULLS**

Cranium

Brow horn core

Orbit

Parietosquamosal
frill

Epoccipital
bone

Nose horn
core

Naris

Mandible

**SKULL AND MANDIBLE
OF TRICERATOPS**

Thick, scaly skin

Epoccipital
bone

Parietosquamosal
frill

Brow horn
(orbital)

Thigh

Nose
horn

Tail

Ankle

Knee

Hindlimb

Nail

Elbow

Forelimb

Wrist

Eye

Naris

Tongue

Toothless
beak

Nose
horn
core

Parietal
fenestra

Epoccipital
bone

Parietosquamosal frill

Supraorbital ridge

Orbit

Naris

Cranium

Mandible

**SKULL AND MANDIBLE
OF STYRACOSAURUS**

Parietosquamosal frill

Anterior horn core

Cranium

Supraorbital ridge

Orbit

Parietal
fenestra

Nose
horn core

Naris

Epoccipital
bone

Rostral bone

Infratemporal
fenestra

Jugal bone

**SKULL OF
EUCENTROSAURUS**

Ilium

Hip joint

Caudal
vertebrae

Ischium

Prepubis

Femur

Knee joint

Fibula

Tibia

Epoccipital bone

Parietal fenestra

Parietosquamosal
frill

Brow
horn core

Nose horn
core

Naris

Horn core

Parietal
fenestra

Cranium

Nasofrontal boss

Orbit

Naris

Epoccipital bone

Rostral
bone

Parietosquamosal frill

Infratemporal fenestra

Jugal bone

Chevron

Neural spine

Ankle joint

Metatarsals

Phalanges

SKULL OF CHASMOSAURUS

SKULL OF PACHYRHINOSAURUS

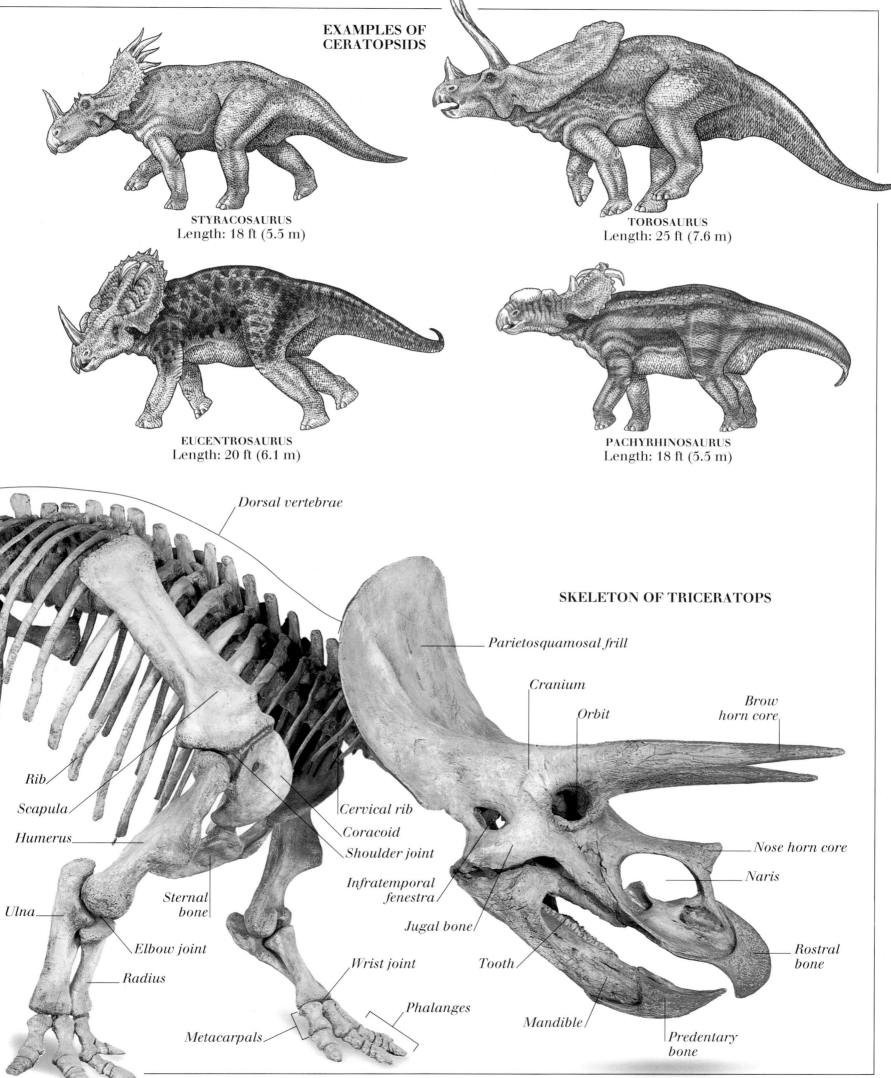

EXAMPLES OF CERATOPSIDS

STYRACOSAURUS
Length: 18 ft (5.5 m)

TOROSAURUS
Length: 25 ft (7.6 m)

EUCENTROSAURUS
Length: 20 ft (6.1 m)

PACHYRHINOSAURUS
Length: 18 ft (5.5 m)

SKELETON OF TRICERATOPS

Dorsal vertebrae

Parietosquamosal frill

Cranium

Orbit

Brow horn core

Rib

Scapula

Humerus

Cervical rib

Coracoid

Shoulder joint

Nose horn core

Ulna

Infratemporal fenestra

Naris

Jugal bone

Sternal bone

Elbow joint

Rostral bone

Radius

Wrist joint

Tooth

Phalanges

Metacarpals

Mandible

Predentary bone

Hands and claws

FOSSIL OF DINOSAUR CLAW

THE HANDS OF CARNIVOROUS (flesh-eating) dinosaurs – *Deinocheirus* and *Baryonyx*, for example – typically had three fingers (although a few had two), each tipped with a sharp claw. Many carnivorous dinosaurs also had opposable fingers that enabled them to grasp. They walked on their hind legs, leaving their arms and hands free to attack prey. However, the arms of some carnivores, notably *Tyrannosaurus*, were so short that they did not even reach their mouths. Most herbivores (plant-eaters) had padded hands with four or five fingers, tipped with claws or blunt nails. Many herbivores also had sharp thumb claws for digging or defense. Unlike carnivores, herbivores did not generally have opposable fingers. Although many herbivores – *Iguanodon* and *Prosaurolophus*, for example – had strong, weight-bearing forelimbs, such dinosaurs could also walk or run on their hind legs alone.

EXAMPLES OF DINOSAUR CLAWS

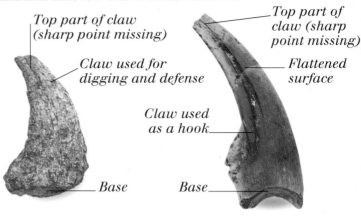

Top part of claw (sharp point missing)

Claw used for digging and defense

Base

MASSOSPONDYLUS THUMB CLAW

Top part of claw (sharp point missing)

Flattened surface

Claw used as a hook

Base

ORNITHOMIMUS FINGER CLAW

Hook shape

Sharp tip

Claw used for catching fish

Base

BARYONYX THUMB CLAW

Top part of claw (sharp point missing)

Claw used for digging and defense

Broad surface

Base

APATOSAURUS THUMB CLAW

SKELETON OF ARMS OF DEINOCHEIRUS

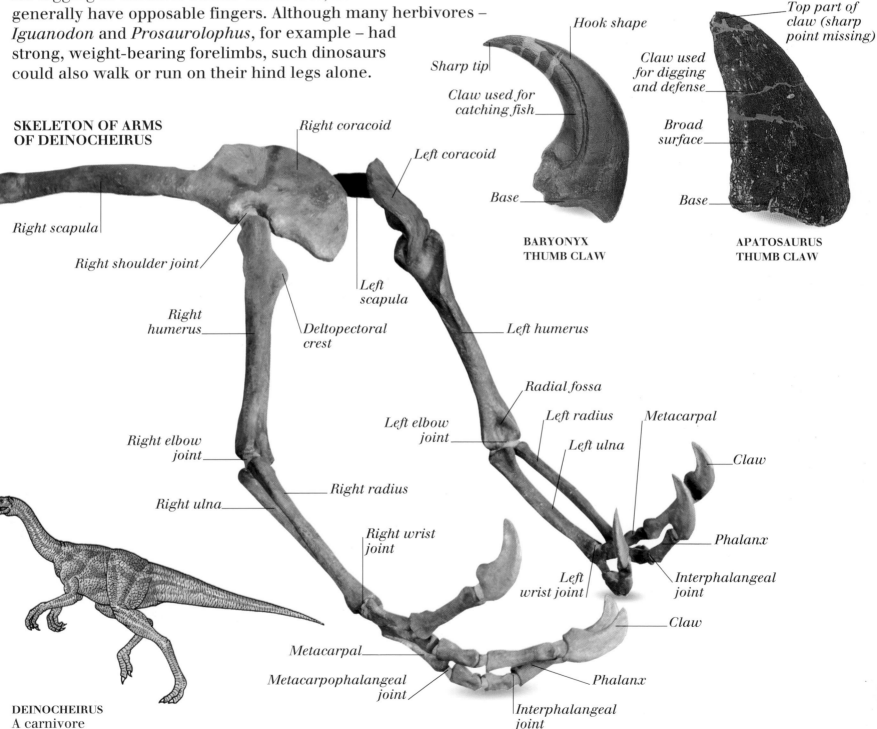

Right coracoid

Left coracoid

Right scapula

Right shoulder joint

Left scapula

Right humerus

Deltopectoral crest

Left humerus

Radial fossa

Left elbow joint

Left radius

Metacarpal

Right elbow joint

Left ulna

Claw

Right radius

Right ulna

Phalanx

Right wrist joint

Left wrist joint

Interphalangeal joint

Claw

Metacarpal

Metacarpophalangeal joint

Phalanx

Interphalangeal joint

DEINOCHEIRUS
A carnivore

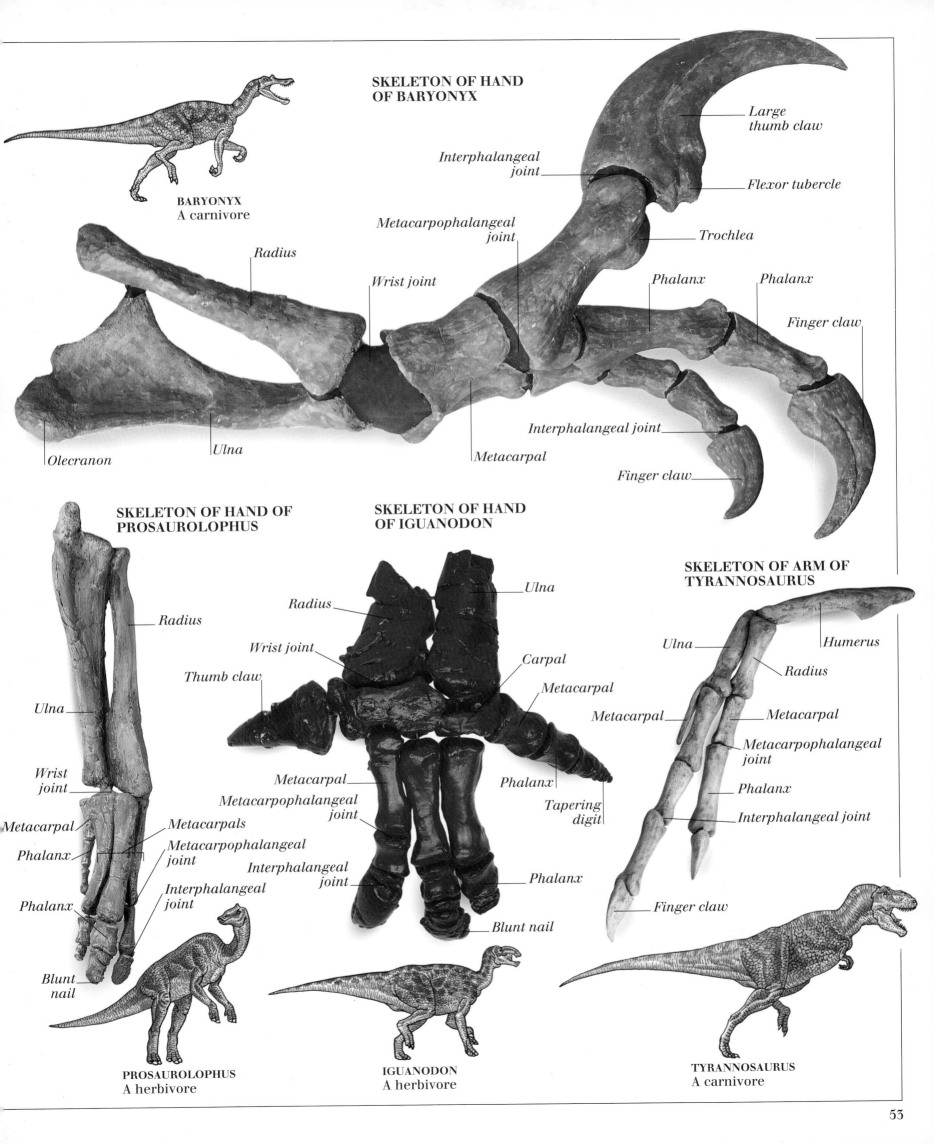

**SKELETON OF HAND
OF BARYONYX**

Large
thumb claw

Interphalangeal
joint

Flexor tubercle

Metacarpophalangeal
joint

Trochlea

Radius

Wrist joint

Phalanx

Phalanx

Finger claw

Olecranon

Ulna

Interphalangeal joint

Metacarpal

Finger claw

BARYONYX
A carnivore

**SKELETON OF HAND OF
PROSAUROLOPHUS**

**SKELETON OF HAND
OF IGUANODON**

**SKELETON OF ARM OF
TYRANNOSAURUS**

Radius

Ulna

Humerus

Radius

Wrist joint

Carpal

Ulna

Thumb claw

Metacarpal

Radius

Ulna

Metacarpal

Metacarpal

Phalanx

Metacarpophalangeal
joint

Metacarpal

Metacarpophalangeal
joint

Phalanx

Phalanx

Interphalangeal
joint

Metacarpals

Tapering
digit

Interphalangeal joint

Metacarpophalangeal
joint

Phalanx

Interphalangeal
joint

Interphalangeal
joint

Phalanx

Finger claw

Phalanx

Blunt
nail

Blunt nail

PROSAUROLOPHUS
A herbivore

IGUANODON
A herbivore

TYRANNOSAURUS
A carnivore

Feet and tracks

**SKELETON OF FOOT
OF PLATEOSAURUS**

Dinosaurs had high ankles and walked on their toes. However, apart from these common characteristics, the feet of dinosaurs were extremely diverse. For example, *Stegosaurus*, a large, heavy dinosaur that walked on all fours (a quadruped), had broad, short, elephant-like feet. In contrast, certain large, heavy, semi-quadrupeds (quadrupedal dinosaurs that sometimes walked or ran on their hind legs), such as *Parasaurolophus* and *Iguanodon*, had longer feet with separate toes. Smaller, lighter dinosaurs that walked on two legs (bipeds), such as *Chirostenotes*, *Compsognathus*, and *Dromiceiomimus*, had relatively long, narrow, birdlike feet. The fossilized tracks of some dinosaurs indicate not only the structure of their feet, but also how they moved. For example, the tracks of *Ornithomimus* confirm that it was bipedal, and also indicate that it was lightweight and could run quickly.

*Imprint of foot
of Ornithomimus*

*Imprint
of toe*

*Imprint
of toe*

Material of cast

**FOOT OF
STEGOSAURUS**

**FOOT OF
COMPSOGNATHUS**

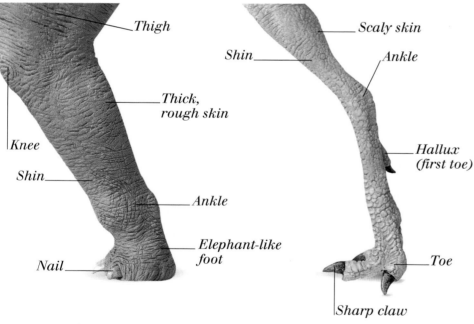

Thigh

*Thick,
rough skin*

Knee

Shin

Nail

Ankle

*Elephant-like
foot*

Scaly skin

Shin

Ankle

*Hallux
(first toe)*

Toe

Sharp claw

**CAST OF FOSSILIZED
IGUANODON TRACK**

*Imprint of
hindfoot of
Iguanodon*

*Material
of cast*

Imprint of toe

STEGOSAURUS
Length: 30 ft (9.1 m)

COMPSOGNATHUS
Length: 28 in (70 cm)

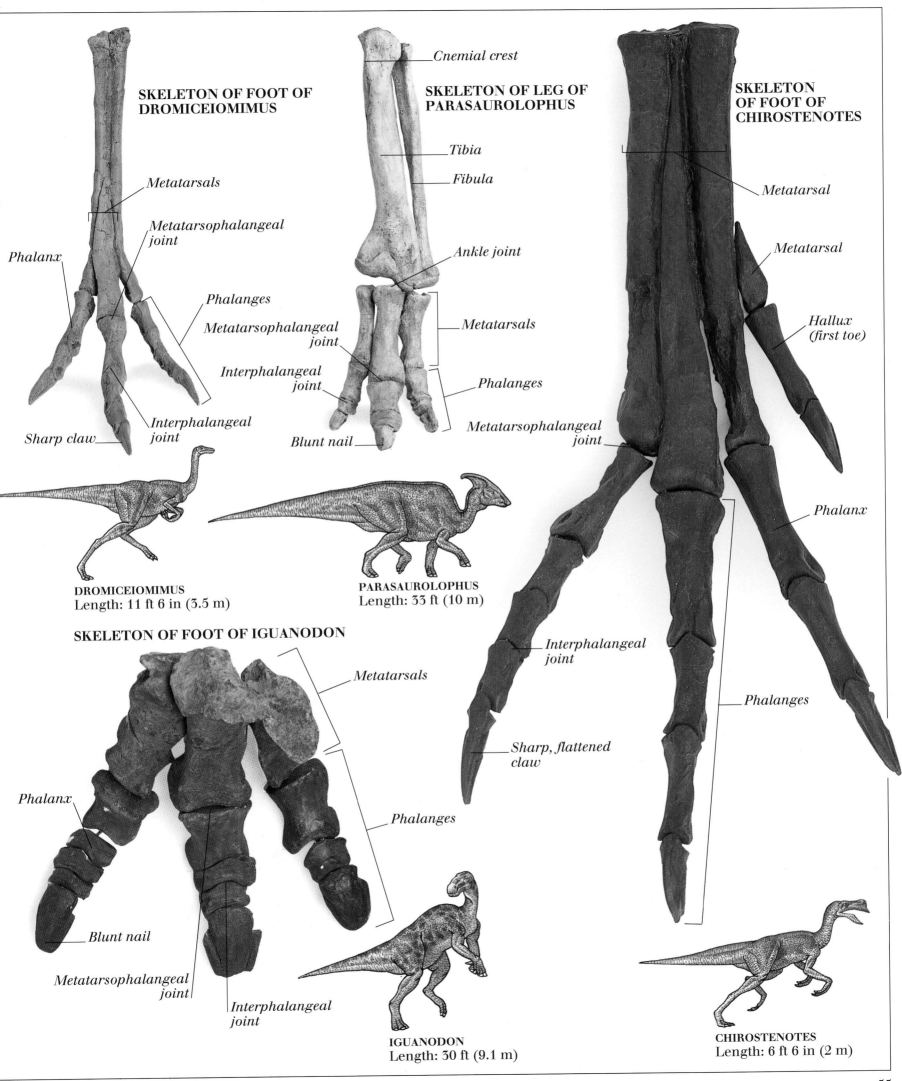

SKELETON OF FOOT OF DROMICEIOMIMUS

Metatarsals

Metatarsophalangeal joint

Phalanx

Phalanges

Metatarsophalangeal joint

Interphalangeal joint

Interphalangeal joint

Sharp claw

SKELETON OF LEG OF PARASAUROLOPHUS

Cnemial crest

Tibia

Fibula

Ankle joint

Metatarsals

Phalanges

Metatarsophalangeal joint

Blunt nail

SKELETON OF FOOT OF CHIROSTENOTES

Metatarsal

Metatarsal

Hallux (first toe)

Phalanx

Interphalangeal joint

Phalanges

Sharp, flattened claw

DROMICEIOMIMUS
Length: 11 ft 6 in (3.5 m)

PARASAUROLOPHUS
Length: 33 ft (10 m)

SKELETON OF FOOT OF IGUANODON

Metatarsals

Phalanx

Phalanges

Blunt nail

Metatarsophalangeal joint

Interphalangeal joint

IGUANODON
Length: 30 ft (9.1 m)

CHIROSTENOTES
Length: 6 ft 6 in (2 m)

Dinosaur relatives

MOST DINOSAURS BECAME EXTINCT about 65 million years ago. However, modern birds are considered to be living dinosaurs, while crocodiles are generally thought to be the dinosaurs' closest living relatives. It has been suggested that birds and dinosaurs diverged from a common ancestor during the Early Jurassic (208–188 million years ago). However, the most widely accepted view is that birds evolved from small, bipedal (two-legged) dinosaurs, such as *Deinonychus*. The principal evidence for this relationship is the similarity between the limb bones of *Coelophysis*, *Archaeopteryx* (the oldest known bird), and modern birds: all have forelimbs with three digits, and hindlimbs with four toes, one of which is a reversed hallux (first toe). Possibly descended from *Archaeopteryx* were *Ichthyornis* and *Hesperornis*, both birds of the Late Cretaceous (97.5–65 million years ago), and the more modern (but extinct) *Diatryma*, *Paleospheniscus,* and *Presbyornis*, as well as present-day birds. Crocodiles are only remotely related to the dinosaurs, because the two groups evolved along different lines after splitting off from a common ancestral group during the Early Triassic (248–243 million years ago).

FOSSIL OF A BIRD'S FEATHER

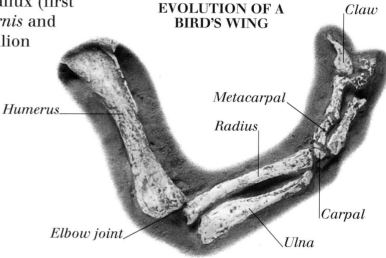

HESPERORNIS REGALIS
Length: 6 ft (1.8 m)

EVOLUTION OF A BIRD'S WING

Claw

Humerus

Metacarpal

Radius

Carpal

Elbow joint

Ulna

SKELETON OF FORELIMB OF COELOPHYSIS

EXTERNAL FEATURES OF ARCHAEOPTERYX

Claw

Finger

Eye

Beak

Feather

Neck

Feather

Bony tail core

Hindlimb

Knee

Tail feather

Ankle

Reversed hallux (first toe)

Toe

Claw

Carpal

Metacarpal

Radius

Phalanx

Humerus

Phalanx

Metacarpal

Claw

Ulna

Elbow joint

SKELETON OF WING OF ARCHAEOPTERYX

Phalanx

Radius

Carpometacarpus

Humerus

Phalanx

Ulna

Phalanx

Elbow joint

Phalanx

SKELETON OF WING OF MODERN BIRD

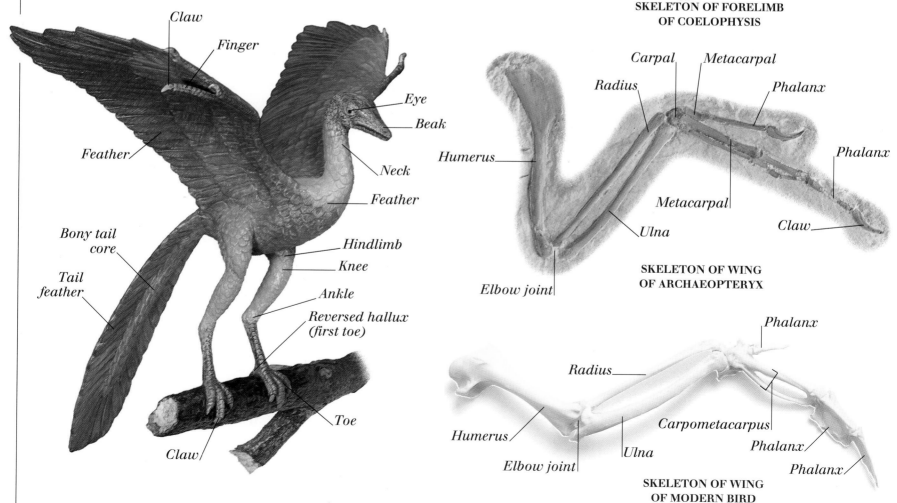

EXAMPLES OF EXTINCT BIRDS

PRESBYORNIS PERVETUS
Height: 3 ft 3 in (1 m)

PALEOSPHENISCUS PATAGONICUS
Height: 26 in (66 cm)

ICHTHYORNIS DISPAR
Length: 8 in (20 cm)

DIATRYMA GIGANTEA
Height: 7 ft (2.1 m)

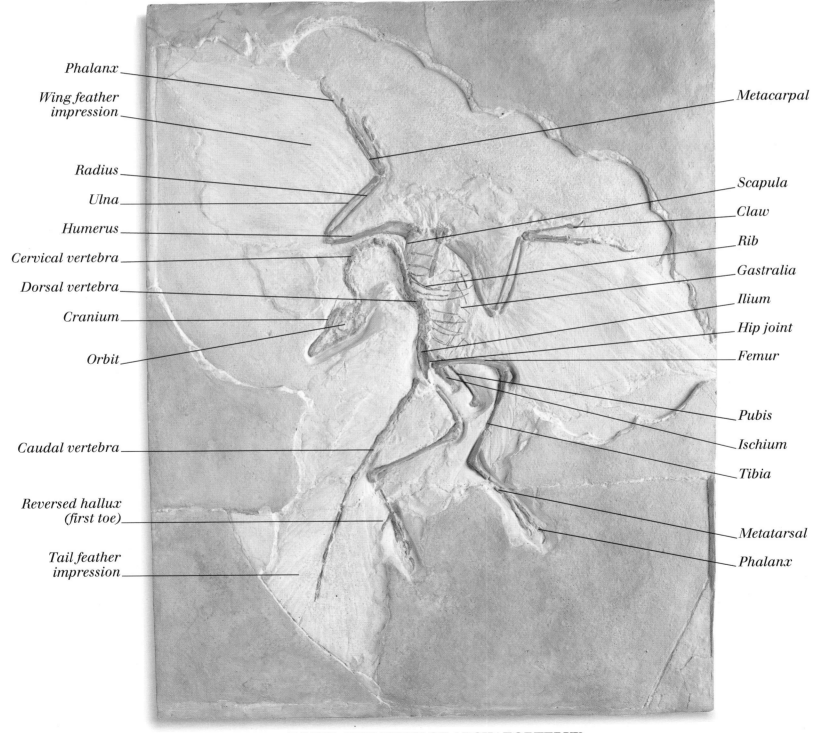

Phalanx

Wing feather impression

Radius

Ulna

Humerus

Cervical vertebra

Dorsal vertebra

Cranium

Orbit

Caudal vertebra

Reversed hallux (first toe)

Tail feather impression

Metacarpal

Scapula

Claw

Rib

Gastralia

Ilium

Hip joint

Femur

Pubis

Ischium

Tibia

Metatarsal

Phalanx

FOSSIL SKELETON OF ARCHAEOPTERYX

Dinosaur classification

THE CLASSIFICATION OF DINOSAURS is controversial and is continually being revised in the light of new fossil finds and reinterpretations of existing evidence. There are also a number of different methods of classification. The method used here is based on inherited features shared by members of a group but not by any members in other groups. According to this classification, all dinosaurs and their relatives belong to the major group Archosauria (ruling reptiles). The Archosauria can be split into two main divisions: primitive archosaurs, which include Proterosuchia, Erythrosuchia, *Euparkeria*, and Crurotarsi; and ornithodiran archosaurs, which include Pterosauria, *Lagosuchus*, and the Dinosauria. The Dinosauria ("true" dinosaurs) can be divided in turn into three groups: Herrerasauria (early predatory dinosaurs), Saurischia (lizard-hipped dinosaurs), and Ornithischia (bird-hipped dinosaurs). Each group can then be subdivided down to the levels of families (with names ending in "-idae"), genera (indicated by italics in this chart), and species.

KEY

ARCHOSAURS (RULING REPTILES)

PRIMITIVE ARCHOSAURS

ORNITHODIRAN ARCHOSAURS

FLYING ARCHOSAURS

DINOSAUR-LIKE ARCHOSAURS

DINOSAURS

EARLY PREDATORY DINOSAURS

LIZARD-HIPPED DINOSAURS

BIRD-HIPPED DINOSAURS

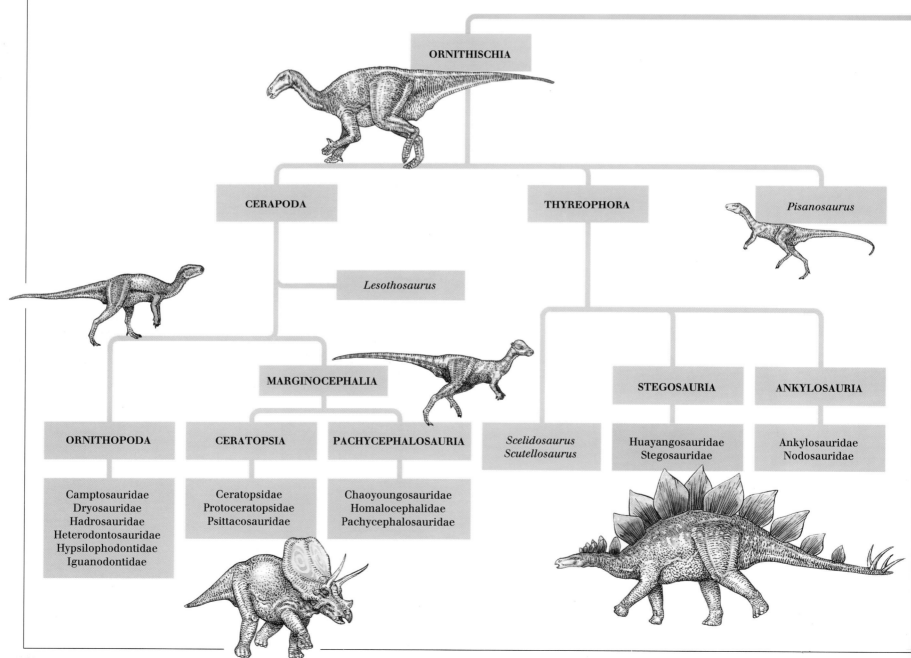

ORNITHISCHIA

CERAPODA

THYREOPHORA

Pisanosaurus

Lesothosaurus

MARGINOCEPHALIA

STEGOSAURIA

ANKYLOSAURIA

ORNITHOPODA

CERATOPSIA

PACHYCEPHALOSAURIA

Scelidosaurus
Scutellosaurus

Huayangosauridae
Stegosauridae

Ankylosauridae
Nodosauridae

Camptosauridae
Dryosauridae
Hadrosauridae
Heterodontosauridae
Hypsilophodontidae
Iguanodontidae

Ceratopsidae
Protoceratopsidae
Psittacosauridae

Chaoyoungosauridae
Homalocephalidae
Pachycephalosauridae

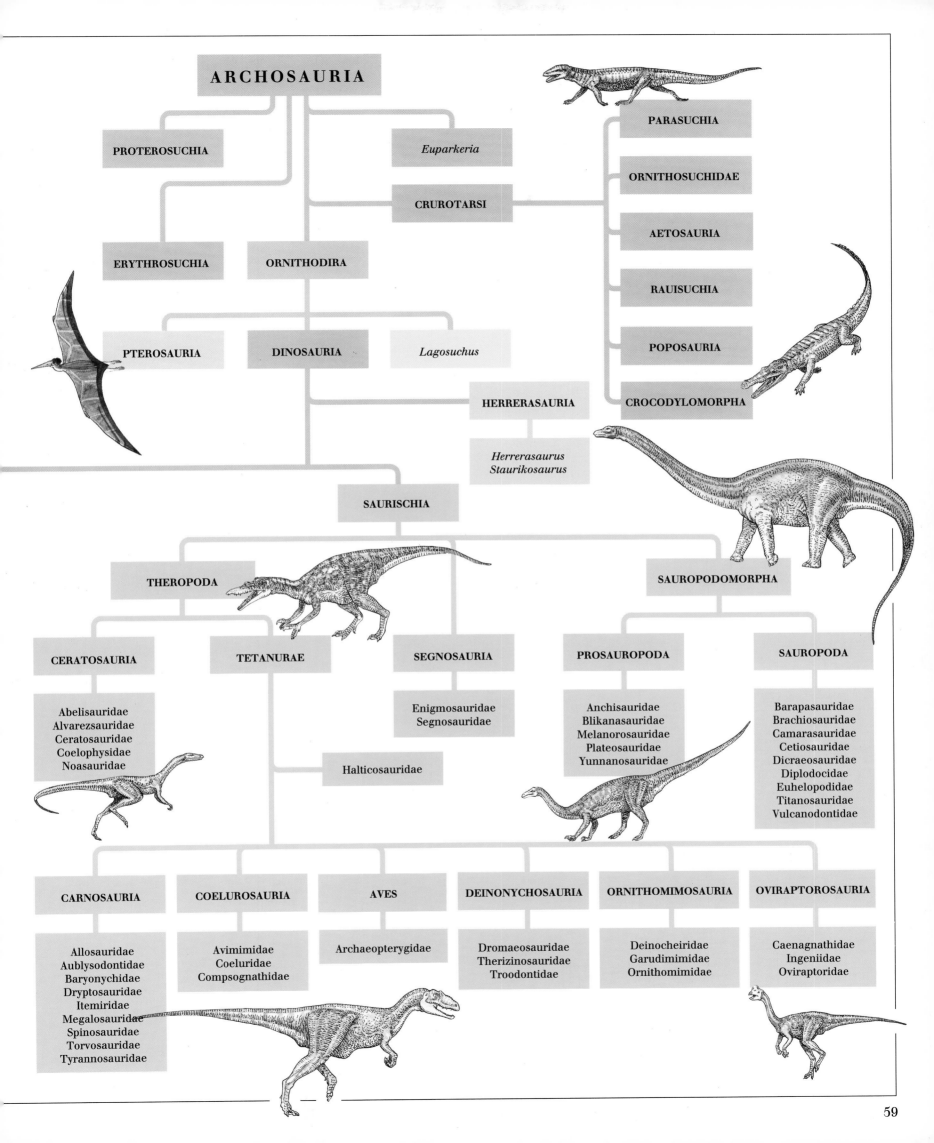

ARCHOSAURIA

PROTEROSUCHIA

Euparkeria

PARASUCHIA

ORNITHOSUCHIDAE

CRUROTARSI

AETOSAURIA

RAUISUCHIA

ERYTHROSUCHIA

ORNITHODIRA

POPOSAURIA

PTEROSAURIA

DINOSAURIA

Lagosuchus

CROCODYLOMORPHA

HERRERASAURIA

Herrerasaurus
Staurikosaurus

SAURISCHIA

THEROPODA

SAUROPODOMORPHA

CERATOSAURIA

TETANURAE

SEGNOSAURIA

PROSAUROPODA

SAUROPODA

Abelisauridae
Alvarezsauridae
Ceratosauridae
Coelophysidae
Noasauridae

Enigmosauridae
Segnosauridae

Anchisauridae
Blikanasauridae
Melanorosauridae
Plateosauridae
Yunnanosauridae

Barapasauridae
Brachiosauridae
Camarasauridae
Cetiosauridae
Dicraeosauridae
Diplodocidae
Euhelopodidae
Titanosauridae
Vulcanodontidae

Halticosauridae

CARNOSAURIA

COELUROSAURIA

AVES

DEINONYCHOSAURIA

ORNITHOMIMOSAURIA

OVIRAPTOROSAURIA

Allosauridae
Aublysodontidae
Baryonychidae
Dryptosauridae
Itemiridae
Megalosauridae
Spinosauridae
Torvosauridae
Tyrannosauridae

Avimimidae
Coeluridae
Compsognathidae

Archaeopterygidae

Dromaeosauridae
Therizinosauridae
Troodontidae

Deinocheiridae
Garudimimidae
Ornithomimidae

Caenagnathidae
Ingeniidae
Oviraptoridae

Index

Acknowledgments

Dorling Kindersley would like to thank:
Dr. Monty Reid, Andrew Neuman, and the staff at the Royal Tyrrell Museum of Palaeontology, Drumheller, Alberta; Dr. Angela Milner and the staff at the Department of Palaeontology, the Natural History Museum, London; Professor W. Ziegler and the staff, in particular Michael Loderstaedt, at the Naturmuseum Senckenburg, Frankfurt; Dr. Alexander Liebau, Axel Hunghrebüller, Reiner Schoch, and the staff at the Institut und Museum für Geologie und Paläontologie der Universität, Tübingen; Rupert Wild at the Institut für Paläontologie, Staatliches Museum für Naturkunde, Stuttgart; Dr. Scheiber, the Stadtmuseum, Nördlingen; Professor Dr. Dietrich Herm, Staatssammlung für Paläontologie und Historische Geologie, München; Dr. Michael Keith-Lucas, Department of Botany, University of Reading; Dr. Richard Walker. For skeletons: the Royal Tyrrell Museum of Palaeontology, Alberta: *Dromaeosaurus* pp. 16-17, *Gryposaurus* pp. 38-39, *Heterodontosaurus* p. 35, *Maiasaura* p. 58, *Ornitholestes* p. 15, *Ornithomimus* pp. 18-19, *Parasaurolophus* pp. 40-41, *Stegoceras* pp. 46-47,

Struthiomimus p. 19, *Triceratops* pp. 50-51; Naturmuseum Senckenberg, Frankfurt: *Archaeopteryx* p. 57, *Diplodocus* pp. 28-29, *Iguanodon* p. 36, *Tyrannosaurus* pp. 22-23, *Stegosaurus* p. 43; Institut und Museum für Geologie und Paläontologie der Universität Tübingen: *Plateosaurus* pp. 24-25, *Kentrosaurus* p. 43; the Natural History Museum, London: *Baryonyx* p. 21, *Tuojiangosaurus* p. 43; Staatliches Museum für Naturkunde, Stuttgart: *Coelophysis* p. 15, *Compsognathus* p. 14; American Museum of Natural History, New York: *Protoceratops* pp. 48-49

Model makers:
John Holmes: *Euoplocephalus* pp. 44-45, *Gallimimus* pp. 18-19, *Hypsilophodon* pp. 34-35; Roby Braun: *Anchisaurus* pp. 24-25, *Compsognathus* pp. 14-15, *Stegosaurus* pp. 42-43; Centaur Studios: *Barosaurus* pp. 28-29, *Baryonyx* pp. 20-21, *Brachiosaurus* pp. 26-27, *Corythosaurus* pp. 40-41, *Iguanodon* pp. 36-37, *Triceratops* p. 50; David Donkin: Cretaceous globe p. 13, Jurassic globe p. 11, Triassic globe p. 9

Additional consultancy:
William Lindsay; Lowell Dingus (American Museum of Natural History, New York)

Additional photography:
John Downs, Tim Parmenter, and Colin Keates (Natural History Museum, London); Lynton Gardiner (American Museum of Natural History, New York); Steve Gorton; Dave King

Photographic assistance:
Kevin Zak; Gary Ombler

Additional design assistance:
Lesley Betts; Christina Betts

Additional editorial assistance:
Jacqui Hand; Jeanette Cossar

Index:
Kay Wright